The Cradle of Violence

Essays on Psychiatry, Psychoanalysis and Literature

Forensic Focus 2

The Cradle of Violence
Essays on Psychiatry, Psychoanalysis and Literature

Stephen Wilson

Jessica Kingsley Publishers
London and Bristol, Pennsylvania

The right of Stephen Wilson to be identified as author of this work has been asserted by him in accordance with the Copyright, Designs and Patents Act 1988.

First published in the United Kingdom in 1995 by
Jessica Kingsley Publishers Ltd
116 Pentonville Road
London N1 9JB, England
and
1900 Frost Road, Suite 101
Bristol, PA 19007, U S A

Library of Congress Cataloging in Publication Data
A CIP catalogue record for this book is available from the Library of Congress
Wilson, Stephen (Stephen Robert), 1944-
The cradle of violence : essays on psychiatry, psychoanalysis and
literature / Stephen Wilson.
p.   cm. -- (Forensic focus : 2)
Includes bibliographical references and Index.
ISBN 1-85302-306-X (pb)
1. Psychiatry. 2. Psychoanalysis and literature. 3. Violence -
Psychological aspects. I. Title II. Series.
RC454.4.W547 1995
616.89--dc20   95-14278
                                                                          CIP

British Library Cataloguing in Publication Data
A CIP catalogue record for this book is available from the British Library

ISBN 1 85302 306 X

Printed and Bound in Great Britain by
Cromwell Press, Melksham, Wiltshire

Contents

To my family, and to the memory of my father Lewis Wilson

Acknowledgements

Dr Kate Wilson, my wife, colleague and friend, has encouraged these essays through all the stages of their preparation. Drs David Clark and Junichi Suzuki in Cambridge and Bertram Mandelbrote, Anthony Storr and Peter Agulnik in Oxford nurtured my development as a psychiatrist. Professor George Brown sharpened my understanding of research methods in the Social Sciences, as did Mr David Kennard with whom I collaborated in fruitful work on therapeutic communities. Dr Donald Meltzer made the value of Psychoanalysis accessible to me. Thanks are also due to the many friends, teachers, students and patients, who over the years have helped me to learn. Dr Murray Cox and Ms Jessica Kingsley, have generously shared their store of enthusiasm.

Foreword

A Foreword is defined as 'A word said before something else; hence, a preface' (OED). It might reasonably be suggested that a pre-preface before that written by the author would be superfluous. Yet the etymology of the very word 'superfluous' takes us directly to one of the central concerns of the book. To be 'superfluous' implies a fluid abundance which 'flows over'; an intermingling of streaming streams. These essays deal with currents and counter-currents; the flow of ideas and skills; tributary notions and mainstream issues, as well as offering the reader meandering poetic reverie and the psychological implications of retardation or acceleration during transit of the birth canal. Stephen Wilson describes the various chapters as 'meanders'. Here again the history of a word proves to be so informative. The Meander was originally the name of a river in Phrygia. The noun has metamorphosed and become adjectival of a mode of flowing, as well as finding its commonest existence as a verb. In the same way, 'meanders' will enable the reader to linger in some areas of his professional landscape which he might otherwise have rushed through. It seems almost miraculous to discover that recent rifting has changed the ancient meandering Meander into a water course that offers 'easy corridors' of access. There is no reason why this book should not do the same thing. Streams of consciousness and unconsciousness, theory and practice, the general and the particular, the individual and the group, fact and fiction, the literal and the metaphorical foam together, like waters beneath a weir.

The wide compass of the material demonstrates the frequent confluence of such interests within the ambit of forensic psychotherapy. At the same time, the book urges the reader to maintain discriminatory distance and not to fuse, and thus confuse, dynamic energies which are on-stream – to adopt a current idiom.

All in all, it stimulates thought and encourages us to remain up-stream of foreclosure. But, when the time comes to formulate a psychodynamic assessment of an unstable fluid forensic constellation, these essays will prove to have reinforced our powers of clinical decision-making.

For all these reasons *The Cradle of Violence* is welcome and can expect to feel on home ground in the Forensic Focus series.

Murray Cox
June 1995

Preface

I regard these essays written over a period of fifteen years, some originating as lectures, others as chapters in books, papers in professional journals or articles in magazines, as meanders. But like all streams, the course is not entirely random. It has been shaped by the exigencies of my daily work, and by the enduring passions of literature and psychoanalysis. I have been fortunate in having had the opportunity to practice in a variety of settings: clinical and research, National Health Service and private practice, hospital, primary care and university.

None of this could be described as mainstream forensic psychotherapy, yet almost every essay touches on the subject – the murderous impulse in a dream, a novelist's work, a GP's surgery, a small child's play, a poet's mind. Thus, contrary perhaps to popular belief, the encounter between psychological medicine and the law is inextricably bound up with the generality of humankind. It is the underside of our 'thin veneer of civilisation', with which both psychoanalysts and writers have been concerned, and it surfaces when conflicts come to be publicly adjudicated.

Forensic psychiatry is forced to address the most fundamental and unyielding of philosophical questions: free will versus determinism, the mind/body problem, the distinction between right and wrong; not in the timeless comfort of the philosopher's armchair but under the urgent constraints of the consulting room and the court of law. It can do with all the help it can get both from science and the humanities.

Stephen Wilson
Oxford, August 1994

Ways of Seeing the Therapeutic Community

INTRODUCTION

During the period following the 1939–45 war, some residential institutions began to be called therapeutic communities. Perhaps because the term was indeterminate, yet had obvious connotations of fellowship, co-operation and salutary intent, it became popular. As the number of therapeutic communities increased, so did diversity of ideas, methods and practices. Institutions ranging from large prisons to small rehabilitation hostels, from psychiatric wards to houses in approved schools, all described themselves with the same name. This chapter attempts to unravel some of the ideas associated with the therapeutic community concept and organise them into several different perspectives. It is hoped that these will provide alternative frames of reference, in which the aims and activities of any particular community can be set.

THE THERAPEUTIC COMMUNITY AS AN ORGANISATIONAL STRUCTURE

Social arrangements which arise at an identifiable point in time and are founded by people with certain purposes in mind, may be called organisations. They are abstract entities, by their nature unobservable, although their effects may be apparent. Nevertheless such social artefacts may be thought of as having structure.

Max Weber (1948) attempted to codify the structural features of organisations. In particular, in his concept of a 'rational bureaucratic organisation', certain elements were fundamental. These included: a clear hierarchy of offices, clear functional specification of each office, impersonal duties and a unified control and disciplinary system, based on a body of rules. For Weber, rationality was essentially the process of applying general rules to particular cases and thus saving effort, by obviating the need to derive a new solution for every problem. It followed that bureaucracy, as a mode of organisation, was particularly antipathetic to the unique treatment of individual cases according to their merit.

Much debate has surrounded the logical status of Weber's model and its relationship to empirical reality. It is probably best considered an 'ideal type', to which real organisations can only approximate. If this is so, mental hospitals as they existed in Britain during the first half of the twentieth century may have provided as close an approximation to a 'rational bureaucracy' as one would wish to find.

Rigidly hierarchical, the patterns of administration and patient care in these institutions were largely based on a nineteenth-century lunacy act, which was rule-bound and punitive. As recently as 1972 the Hospital Advisory Service commented in its Annual Report:

> 'An Advisory Team may be told by senior staff that the hospital is progressive, has modern policies and has done away with outdated practices. In reality the nurses may be spending their time counting knives and forks before locking them away, instituting bathing days for patients, keeping bowel books, shaving all male patients irrespective of their capabilities or needs, and maintaining a patient's day which has not been reviewed in twenty years.'

During the 1950s renewed interest developed in the relationship between the social circumstances of patients and their mental state. The mode of management of a patient was recognised as an important factor in determining his mental well-being. This view, which had been largely obscured following the decline of 'moral treatment', was supported by sociological observations made by several workers in mental hospitals. Goffman in particular was able to link together the concept of bureaucracy as a mode of organisation, with the production of damage to an individual's identity.

In his elaboration of the concept of 'total institution', Goffman (1961) suggested that, in modern society, there was an important division between the spheres of sleep, work and play. Within the bounds of a 'total institution' these barriers were broken down, so that every aspect of life was conducted in the same place under the same single authority. Inside the institution, a small supervisory staff managed a large group of inmates, through a system of inflexible general rules. These were interpreted through strictly regulated channels traversing a large social distance. The effect of this process, Goffman claimed, was nothing less than the destruction of the inmate's 'self', while the prime cause was 'the handling of many human needs by the bureaucratic organisation of whole blocks of people'.

Other aspects of the dysfunctional nature of bureaucracy in mental hospitals were described by Stanton and Schwartz (1954), and Caudill (1958). These studies claimed to demonstrate the harmful effects of covert disagreements between staff members, which were exacerbated by the bureaucratic organisational systems. Bureaucratic structures, according to these authors, blocked communications between occupants of different roles by increasing social distance and providing long hierarchical chains of command along which information had to travel before decisions could be made. Furthermore, through their rigid impersonal role prescriptions, conflicts of feeling among staff members were denied expression, and efforts at greater openness were subject to punitive action. This process, and not the illness, was said to be the cause of much of the disturbed behaviour observed in patients.

The idea of a 'therapeutic community' grew up in this climate of opinion. Its development may thus be seen as a search for a new organisational form, carried out against a background of increasing awareness of the negative effects of bureaucracy, and growing dissatisfaction with this mode of organisation for residential care.

The war years had proved to be a stimulus to innovation. During this period, experiments were carried out by several British military psychiatrists, who attempted to reorganise the social structure of the units for which they were responsible. A reduction in the social distance between patients, nurses and doctors was sought. Maxwell Jones attempted to achieve this in a variety of large unstructured group meetings, in which all members of the unit could participate, and in theory communicate freely. Tom Main (1946) argued the need for the social structure of a hospital to become itself a therapeutic instrument, emphasising the desirability of an emergent structure, rather than a medically dictated authoritarian regime. Further experiments after the war resulted in the establishment of a series of units which shared in general the same principles and mode of functioning.

Several features of these units were distinctive. There was an emphasis on flattening the traditional authority pyramid, so that decision-making and responsibility were shared amongst the members of the community. A non-punitive attitude was taken towards rule infringement, deviancy and impulsive behaviour. Free expression of emotion and the outward manifestation of conflict was encouraged in all community members. Problems, it was hoped, could be resolved by group discussions, occurring in a close-knit and informal context, rather than suppressed by punishment. The optimistic belief that people could learn through participating in such experiences, and benefit from having their own accounts of themselves exposed to redefinition by other group members, was characteristic of the units.

The typical features of a 'therapeutic community' thus appear to represent a polar opposite to Weber's 'rational bureaucracy'. In place of a clear hierarchy of offices there is a deliberate attempt to blur roles and de-emphasise professional qualifications. In place of impersonal duties are obligations to break down formal barriers, mix socially with institutional clients, share facilities and foster interpersonal relationships. Finally, in place of administration based on written documents specifying general rules, an effort is made to deal with each situation as it arises on an *ad hoc* basis.

In this view, the therapeutic community represents a particular mode of organisation, which might be called 'anti-bureaucracy'. Bureaucracy, when applied to human caring institutions, produced Goffman's 'total institution': anti-

bureaucracy might then produce a 'minimal institution' or 'therapeutic community'. Both concepts can be assigned to the same logical category, and be
considered to represent different cells within a typology of residential institutions.

THE THERAPEUTIC COMMUNITY AS AN ORGANISATIONAL FUNCTION

In contrast to the structural perspective, in which the therapeutic community
emerges as an anti-bureaucratic institution, attention can be focused upon the
therapeutic function.

Here, a community may be any group of people who come together regularly
and often in the same place, and hold systematic expectations of each other. A
community aspires to be therapeutic if it defines its goals as therapeutic. Wide
variation in this definition may occur so that psychotherapeutic, rehabilitative,
educational and political goals, or combinations of these, may be adopted.
Whichever way the therapeutic function is defined, the formal structure of such
communities remains theoretically unspecified.

It therefore becomes possible to think in terms of a variety of therapeutic
environments, distinguished by their functional aims. An optimum structure
might then exist, which maximally facilitated a given function for a particular
set of individuals. The breadth of this view depends upon the extent to which
the term 'therapeutic' is stretched. In its widest sense the concept degenerates
into meaninglessness. If a narrow view is taken, a legitimate question arises as to
the way in which an organisation might promote a particular function for its
members.

A heuristic model for the psychotherapeutic function of a community can be
derived from the psychoanalytic understanding of institutional relationships. The
phenomena associated with transference, which consist of a re-enactment of
infantile love situations in later adult relationships, were recognised by Freud to
be easily observable in psychiatric institutions. In such places, he remarked:

> 'We can observe transference occurring with the greatest intensity and in
> the most unworthy forms, extending to nothing less than mental bondage,
> and moreover showing the plainest erotic colouring.' (Freud 1912a)

Events occurring in such institutions can therefore be interpreted in the light of
the transference process. Thus as Freud (1912a) pointed out, patients who leave
in an unchanged or relapsed condition may be under the influence of a negative
transference. These people have presumably projected into the institutional staff
a series of hostile psychical prototypes. Others who remain institutionalised for
long periods of time may, Freud suggested, be under the dominance of a
glossed-over erotic transference.

The understanding of institutional relationships in terms of transference has
been developed further by Elliot Jaques, with the help of Melanie Klein's

elaboration of the concept. In her view (1952), transference originated in the same processes of projection and introjection which originally determined early infantile object relationships, and gave rise to the generation of an internal phantasy world. According to Jaques (1955), institutions may also be thought of as having an unconsciously agreed phantasy form and content, consisting of shared internal world elements amongst their members. Unconscious co-operation, he suggested, might give rise to institutionalised roles whereby 'occupants are sanctioned from, or required to take into themselves, the projected objects or impulses of other members'. Within institutions, then, aspects of the early transference relationship, which may be thought of as widely dispersed in the world at large, may be gathered together and organised into a phantasy structure which underpins the overt formal role structure.

The unconscious organisation of such a system of social defences has been described by Isabel Menzies (1960) in the nursing service of a general hospital. In her view the organisation of social defences was itself capable of enforcing the introjection of particular defence mechanisms, thus interfering with an individual's capacity for creative development and personal maturation. The coercive power of the system of conventions and expectations attached to certain roles appears to be capable of overriding individual defence systems, which seem fragile in comparison with the organisational system.

If this is so, and social defence systems are capable of radically interfering with the internal psychic structure of an individual, the possibility arises that a social system might be devised in which psychological growth is promoted rather than inhibited. The structure of the institution might then encourage the introjection of creative objects, rather than their projection and ultimate loss.

The 'therapeutic community' is thus generated in principle from the conception of institutionally structured psycho-dynamics. What the empirical structure of such a community might be remains an open question.

A hierarchical model may then be considered which incorporates some, but not all the features of bureaucracy. This type of community is represented by Synanon and its offshoots which grew up in California during the 1960s. Rooted in the self-help movement, Synanon (Yablonsky 1965) resulted from the initiative of an ex-alcoholic, who allowed a group of addicts to squat in his apartment, and became their leader.

The atmosphere and philosophy of these programmes is different, even antipathetic to, the democratic ideology. On admission a new resident will be required to sever all his ties with the outside world. He will live and work with other residents, occupying a position in a formal hierarchy, with graded degrees of responsibility. Upward mobility through the hierarchy is seen to be possible, and is rewarded with increased status. At first, however, a new member is regarded as emotionally childlike, having to learn responsibility and earn rights and privileges.

Life within the hostel is circumscribed by a series of simple norms which are embodied in strictly enforced rules. It is incumbent upon all residents to scrutinise each others' behaviour and ensure that it conforms to the community morality. Everybody has a duty to report rule infringement, which is considered to be a sign of responsible friendship to the rule breaker. In this environment, dominated by peer-group surveillance, discovery is inevitable and a formidable array of sanctions exists which may be applied to those who deviate. These include: verbal reprimands, demotion in the hierarchy, bans on social communication, and the use of humiliation and ridicule.

In this kind of community, which is anything but permissive and indeed shares much in common with Communist thought-reform programmes, expectations both in relation to the giving and receiving of authoritative instructions are clear cut. In spite of the ferocity of the sanctions, the narrow social distance between staff and inmates seems to ensure that an institutional underworld dedicated to undermining the staff morality does not emerge. Staff members encourage idealisation and actively exhort new recruits to emulate their example.

The rigid structure of the community seems to have the effect of enforcing the distribution of 'internal objects' along particular channels. Transference is highly focused in the staff, who come to represent health and the possibility of giving up addiction. Hostile and destructive impulses are acknowledged and believed to be expunged through a cathartic process of shouting and cursing, with which every encounter group begins.

The fact that the community is cut off from the outside world, that initial regression is encouraged, followed by a step-by-step progression up a ladder of status and responsibility, at the top of which presides an idealised director, seems to make it into a symbolic paradigm for moral regeneration. The powerful force of social pressure, demanding to regulate the direction of transference, is, however, rejected by many in the initial stages; they may complain that they are being infantilised or depersonalised.

People who remain for long periods of time in such programmes, however, often experience a strong sense of internal change. This may be expressed afterwards as a feeling that they have acquired self-respect, which they need to guard carefully. A sense of gratitude to the programme is often present, together with a feeling that they have begun to develop their full potential. They may feel an increased capacity for love, affection and friendship as well as guilt and regret. There seems good reason to believe that for these people, membership of the community has served a therapeutic function.

THE THERAPEUTIC COMMUNITY AS AN ORGANISATIONAL CULTURE

When the formal structure of a series of collectivities is held constant, wide variations remain in their level of functioning. Thus morale in different army units has been noted to fluctuate, although formal role relationships and external situation appear to be controlled. Conversely morale may be consistently high in both 'democratic' and 'hierarchical' therapeutic communities, although the formal structure varies considerably.

The importance of informal relationships in determining the 'culture' of an organisation has been emphasised by many writers. When rules are present they may, as Gouldner (1954) suggested, be used as the 'chips' with which higher- and lower-level personnel bargain over the minimum level of acceptable performance. Where they are absent, rules may in fact be instigated at a relatively low level in the hierarchy. Thus Brown (1972) has commented on the welter of routines found in mental hospitals:

'There is little reason to believe that more than a handful of routines were imposed from "outside" the ward itself; and it is unlikely that all could be explained in terms of the exigencies of caring for a large number of patients. Certainly they were not particularly efficient; and indeed some practices seemed no more than a self-imposed search for order on the part of the staff.' (p.2)

While the therapeutic function of a community may therefore be contingent upon its formal structure, this is clearly not the only, nor necessarily the principal, factor to be taken into consideration.

The particular set of shared meanings and expectations in regard to the details of role performance on a given unit create its culture and determine its atmosphere. In this sense culture is dynamically conceived, as resulting from a complex process of formal and informal negotiation. The community itself may be thought of as a professionalised locale or geographical arena (Strauss *et al.* 1963) where people come together to carry out their respective purposes. The resultant order varies from day to day, according to the particular combination of rules and policies which currently obtain. This ephemeral order may nevertheless be germane to the therapeutic function. Thus, in 1953 a WHO Expert Committee on Psychiatry commented:

'The most important single factor in the efficacy of the treatment given in a mental hospital, appears to the committee to be an intangible element which can only be described as its atmosphere.' (p.17)

In this view of the therapeutic community the emphasis lies on the creation of a therapeutic 'culture', a set of shared symbols and meanings which give body and depth to the sketchy outlines of the formal structure. The process of constructing such a culture is not only influenced by internal organisational factors, but also by powerful external factors. Membership of professional organisations, trade unions, communal and family group ties, social class and status all play a part. Indeed Crozier (1965) found that work satisfaction within an organisation was determined more by the congruence between class situation outside and the prestige of a given job within, than by any other factor.

The creation of a therapeutic culture is thus problematic, since many of the variables which appear to be important in influencing the process cannot be manipulated. The recognition of the importance of such external variables underlies the attempt to apply a systems approach to the conceptualisation of a therapeutic community.

THE THERAPEUTIC COMMUNITY AS AN ORGANISATIONAL SYSTEM

In this view, organisations are considered to be complex combinations of parts, which go to make up a whole. The system is located in a larger environment, which generates its input and accommodates its output. The individual living or working within an organisation is himself conceived as a low-level sub-system forming one component of a higher-level system. The term therapeutic community has then been taken to refer to a system for change (Jones 1974) which is equated with an 'open system'. Such a system is one whose strategy for adaptation to its environment is focused less on erecting defences against penetration from the outside world and more on 'becoming competent in controlling the external and internal environment so that its objectives are achieved' (Argyris 1970). Social system clinicians may then address themselves to the optimal functioning of the system as a whole, as well as the diagnosis and treatment of individual patients (Greenblatt 1972).

This functional perspective fits well in the biological sphere and is therefore perhaps attractive to medically trained psychiatrists. It is easy to view organisms as functioning systems of organs and organelles. In humans, the skin forms a convenient boundary around the whole system; and a consensus on the value of life itself sets limits for the definition of normative physiological functioning.

The transposition of this frame of reference to social organisations, however, produces many fundamental difficulties. In the first place, organisational boundaries are not clear cut. Since all systems are themselves to be considered the units or elements of higher-level systems, an infinite progression exists whereby in principle the satisfactory functioning of one system may always be shown to be dysfunctional for some larger system. Ultimately no community may then be therapeutic unless it fits harmonically with a therapeutic universe.

Second, there is a danger that the *status quo* of a given community will be taken to represent the optimum or only possible reality. All observable phenomena may then be interpreted as performing some essential function for the system.

This can be seen in Parsons's model of the mental hospital, which virtually turns the 'total institution' on its head. The hospital remains a place which is isolated and all-encompassing, yet the degradation and disturbing damage to identity associated with Goffman's picture disappear. In place of references to concentration camps and army barracks, Parsons (1957) finds similarities with church and kinship units. Degradation ceremonies become 'initial socialisation', an essential prerequisite to therapy, and the loss of personal autonomy is elevated to a major system need. Far from being incompatible with the family, the mental hospital is seen by Parsons as a model of family life, necessarily producing, as part of its therapeutic function, 'a situation similar to that of the child in the family'.

In the third place, the continued life of any particular organisation is not always valued equally by its components. Functions must be related to the achievement of specific goals and these may differ amongst individuals or groups within the organisation. Implicit in the concept of a therapeutic community as an open system is an optimistic assumption that internal dissensus can somehow be modified through increased communication. The system may then reach a healthy equilibrium and function homoeostatically in relation to its wider environment.

A hospital, however, as Etzioni (1960) has stressed, is not one social group to which everybody wants to belong, nor even a small society. Conflict between individuals' purposes and goals may result from objective factors: economic, social or technological, which no amount of increased communication can overcome. In such a situation, attempts to open up communication channels and decrease social distance may simply succeed in laying bare the underlying conflict and exacerbating it.

In reality, there may be no way in which the needs of the different sub-systems can be met which is at the same time equally beneficial to all, and functional for the system as a whole. If the system itself is to become the main object of therapy, the result for the individual may consist of improved 'adjustment' to a particular system, either through coercion or more subtle persuasion. While increased understanding of the events which take place within communities may be provided by the systems approach to thinking about them, it is difficult to see how individual psychological development can be fostered by attempts to actively 'treat' the larger system. In fact it is difficult to see how such attempts can be anything more than normal political activity mystified by the rhetoric of medicine.

CONCLUSION

Four perspectives on the therapeutic community have been delineated: structural, functional, cultural and systems. The structural perspective sees the therapeutic community as a debureaucratised unit. The functional perspective emphasises the therapeutic goal, stressing that different formal structures may be therapeutic for different types of people. The cultural perspective draws attention to the informal aspects of the therapeutic environment which go to make up its atmosphere; and the systems perspective emphasises the interrelatedness of different organisational levels. The perspectives are not mutually exclusive. Their analytical separation may, however, be useful to community members who are trying to orientate themselves in a particular unit.

2

Can Drug Abuse Treatment
Be Adequately Evaluated?

This paper jumps off from the observation that after ten years of experience we are still unable to say whether the treatment given by British Drug Clinics cures addicts or makes them worse! Four categories are created in order to explore possible reasons for this situation. *Descriptive* problems revolve around finding a way to conceptualise drug dependence, to grasp the complexity of different treatments and to formulate meaningful outcome criteria. *Measurement* problems include difficulties in quantification and the creation of operational definitions as well as practical issues connected with establishing the truth. *Design* problems include questions as to the ideal way of discovering the relationship between variables and the compromise forced by practical constraints. *Interpretive* problems include difficulties in arriving at the meaning of results, questions relating to causality and drawing the limits which apply to our conclusions.

There are many problems at a variety of different levels and it may not be astonishing that we are unable to come out with a clear-cut causal statement regarding the efficacy of drug abuse treatment. The conditions under which a given evaluative study is to be considered 'adequate' remain a matter of taste.

CAN DRUG ABUSE TREATMENT BE ADEQUATELY EVALUATED?

On the face of it the evaluation of treatment for drug abuse would not seem to present many problems. When we consider the difficulties that exist in achieving diagnostic reliability and validity in other branches of psychiatry or in establishing the criteria for successful treatment, shouldn't the problem of the research worker in this field pale into insignificance? Surely, a naive observer would argue, it is easy enough to ascertain whether or not a given group of people is using drugs. All that would then be necessary would be randomly to allocate a sample into a treatment and control group according to the accepted cannons of medical research and to compare the outcome of the two groups.

In practice, as we know, things are not quite so simple. In a recent review of policies on opiate addiction Griffith Edwards (1979) noted that we were still unable to say whether the treatment given by British Drug Clinics caused addicts to stop using drugs or whether it actually delayed their recovery! As he put it, '... rather astonishingly and after ten years the most crucial assumption of treatment policy has not been adequately evaluated'.

In the present paper I set out to consider some of the reasons for this state of affairs. In doing so I shall draw particularly on my experience of attempting to evaluate the work of a therapeutic community (Wilson 1978), but I believe that the issues thrown up are also of more general interest. I should like to discuss four categories of problem, namely descriptive, design, measurement and interpretive.

Descriptive Problems

Under this heading I am thinking about the fundamental difficulties that exist in trying to describe not only the nature of drug abuse but also the methods of treatment and the changes that may occur in an individual during treatment and after discharge.

The problem of defining what a drug is and distinguishing it from, say, food or poison has been recognised for some time. The term 'substance', which means anything, is now often used instead of 'drug'. Unfortunately, we are immediately confronted by a new problem – how to differentiate anything-use from anything-abuse! The distinction is far from academic since it forms the basis for the selection of the populations which we investigate. The continued and regular need for something, the subjective yearning and pining for it in its absence, even the presence of psychological disorganisation accompanied by physiological changes (withdrawal symptoms) do not seem adequate criteria for this purpose. All these might conceivably be present in a rejected lover, a bereaved spouse or an infant being weaned from the breast. In other words, I believe that we are confronted at the outset with a qualitative problem concerning the meaning of an individual's drug use which cannot be resolved by reference to external behaviour or biological measurements, but is located in the psychological realm. It poses the question, 'How can we distinguish between love and addiction?'

But, supposing that while we ponder this distinction we also look upon drug dependence in a different way, as a behavioural phenomenon or some kind of empirical variable. May we then set out to explore the relationship between drug dependence and family background, criminality, unemployment, institutionalisation, poor housing, treatment modality, a Conservative government and so on? We find ourselves faced with a universe of possible variables and we then have to choose a set of variables to describe the outcome and another set of variables to describe the factors which might influence the outcome amongst which the treatment process is to be included.

As far as the outcome is concerned are we to adopt administrative criteria based on notions of cost-effectiveness which may be close to the heart of government departments and funding agencies? Usually some formula can be devised to assess the cost of a given treatment but the danger is that the effectiveness side of the equation will be overlooked so that what is cheap, easily managed and socially non-disruptive becomes synonymous with success. If we wish to pay more attention to individual development should we then take the addict's own subjective criteria, asking him what changes he hoped for and what he feels he has achieved? We may then have to consider the avoidance of a custodial prison sentence as an indicator of success since many new entrants to drug rehabilitation programmes hope for nothing more than this. If an individual has little ambition for himself and wishes only to be allowed free access to his drug of choice and to be left alone by the authorities, this too would have to be considered success. Should we then take the criteria which the staff of a particular programme embrace in order to see whether it is achieving what it sets out to do? We may then find that an unduly rigid set of demands, sometimes charac-terised by the word 'total' as in total honesty or total abstinence, produce an underestimate of the number of people who have been helped by the programme. This situation is particularly notable in studies of therapeutic communities which pay attention only to the number of people who graduate from a programme. Are we then thrown back onto the research worker's own criteria, which he may like to think of as scientific, restricting himself to 'just reporting the facts', such as the responses to psychological questionnaires or follow-up interviews which assess the degree of social isolation and anomie?

In the final analysis, I think the choice of variables to investigate must rest on a value judgement made by the research worker and must therefore be idiosyn-cratic. If drug use is viewed as inherently harmful, then drug abstinence is likely to be considered a sine qua non of successful outcome. If the problem is conceptualised as primarily social, then social adjustment, ability to hold down a job, get on with one's friends and family, and generally 'succeed' in life are likely to be elevated into primary concerns. If the problem is conceptualised as fundamentally psychological, then the outcome will be viewed in terms of individual development and psychological maturation. The continued use of drugs, either illicitly or on prescription as part of a maintenance programme, must then be considered in the light of its meaning for the individual, which may not be self-evident.

It seems common sense for a research worker to pay attention to a broad range of indicators when assessing the response of an addict to a treatment programme and thus to gain a rounded picture of the follow-up situation. I have been tempted to create an index of 'overall success' by collapsing together a series of variables such as improvement on psychological tests, drug use, criminality and employ-ment record. The point I would like to emphasise here is that these things do not necessarily go together and may even be mutually contradictory. Drug abstinence may be achieved at the expense of psychological development so that an individual substitutes for his addiction what is in fact an obsessional abstinence neurosis accompanied by a phobic reaction to drugs. Social success may be achieved together with or as a result of the use of drugs, and psychological maturation may put an individual into conflict with prevailing social values and therefore militate against social adjustment.

Similarly, when we come to describe the treatment of drug abuse we find a complex set of factors and we have to decide whether it is appropriate to lump them together. For example, one might consider a therapeutic community simply as residential rehabilitation in which the detoxified addict is separated from his usual social context for a certain period of time. One might feel that the social structure, either hierarchical or democratic, was a potent therapeutic force or there might be particular forms of therapy, such as encounter groups or yoga, which could be investigated in their own right. It might be felt that everything depended on the personalities of the staff or that nothing much depended on the personalities of the staff providing that they had been trained in the correct way. If we take any particular community, we find a specific combination of factors which could be regarded as a package. If we are lucky, the contents of the package (staff, social organisation, therapeutic activities) will remain constant for a period, long enough to permit evaluation. More often the situation is nearer to that of a clinical investigator trying to analyse the effect of a medicine whose chemical structure is constantly changing! In any event, we have to be careful to limit our conclusions to the application of this particular combination of measures and if we want to know more specifically which elements are effective, we have to find a way of studying them in purer culture.

Design and Measurement Problems

If, for the time being, we suspend the descriptive difficulties and turn our attention to the relationship between variables, we find a new level of problems. Among the factors which influence outcome we are especially interested in teasing out the role of treatment. We wish to regard the condition of drug addiction as our dependent variable, the treatment as our independent variable and everything else as either extraneous or contingent. In order to perform this kind of causal analysis we have to keep these variables apart so that they do not contaminate each other. But in my experience they have a curious propensity to come together! Thus, if we investigate the social lives of addicts after leaving a therapeutic community we may find that they tend to mix with people who do not take drugs and regard this as an index of successful outcome. It may, however, be argued that the social milieu into which an addict is discharged is bound to influence his drug use and is therefore more correctly seen as a contingent factor influencing the outcome, which must be held constant if we are to achieve a true assessment of treatment efficacy. It may also be taken as a variable more properly ascribed to the treatment process itself since the therapeutic community provides the addict with a new set of friends and enables ex-residents to keep in touch with one another. It seems that in this case the concepts of treatment, outcome and factors related to outcome are inextricably conflated. Any attempt to establish a simple causal connection between treatment and outcome must therefore be doomed to failure.

If, however, we can succeed in isolating our variables, we still have to find a way of exerting control over them. Random allocation from a target population into treatment and control groups appears to be a powerful method but seems almost impossible to apply in practice. Ethical considerations make it difficult to allocate an addict who is seeking treatment into a no-treatment group. Referral agencies who are aware that an experiment is taking place often reduce the number of referrals (Clarke and Cornish 1972) so that sample sizes diminish and the functioning of institutions under investigation can be adversely affected. Furthermore, it is virtually impossible to prevent people from dropping out of a treatment programme, so that even where random allocation has occurred at the beginning of a project, differential attrition in the samples being compared may render them far from equivalent at the time when results are analysed. Finally, of course, the effect of the research process on those being investigated cannot be eliminated by double-blind procedures as in trials of pills, and may even be strong enough to override any differences between treatments under investigation.

It therefore seems more appropriate to use non-experimental designs of the kind more often used in social research. Here the researcher accepts a situation as given and attempts to exert control over the variables in which he is interested by statistical methods such as cross tabulation, the use of partial correlation coefficients or more sophisticated multivariate techniques.

Two difficulties immediately present themselves. In the first place the variables must now be measured on a scale which satisfies the demands of the statistics used. This means that for most analyses involving correlation coefficients an interval scale will be required. The danger now becomes one of imposing such a scale by fiat upon a variable such as drug abuse or contact with friends, which may make nonsense of the qualitative differences between different degrees of involvement by assuming that they are all the same.

Second, if different sub-groups are to be compared and cross-tabulated, the size of the sample needs to be large so that the numbers remaining in each cell when variables are held constant permit meaningful statistical analysis. If a research worker starts off with a sample of, say, one hundred cases, it is likely to shrink during his study by the exclusion of anomalous cases and the practical difficulties involved in follow up. By the time he has controlled for age and sex there will often be less than five cases left in each cell with which to explore the relationship between treatment and outcome. These methods which are useful in large-scale social surveys are therefore of very limited value in projects with small samples.

Another difficulty which crops up in the design of follow-up studies concerns time. Often there is limited time available in which to carry out the study, time needs to be allowed for the treatment to occur and further time is then necessary in order to see whether addicts relapse. If addicts are followed up too quickly a distorted picture may be obtained, people who are going to relapse may not yet have done so or, conversely, ex-addicts leaving a therapeutic community may not have had time to demonstrate that they can live a truly independent existence. On the other hand, if addicts are followed up after, say, twenty years, as Vaillant (1973) has done, the influence of post-treatment intervening variables must be incalculable and furthermore the results may be of little practical relevance to contemporary populations of drug users which are demographically quite different.

There is also a danger that the particular time at which a person seeks or is coerced into a treatment programme represents a low point in the context of their drug career. If criminal conviction or peak levels of drug use are systematically related to admission to a treatment programme, there is a built-in bias towards a post-treatment reduction in convictions and drug use. Similarly, if scores on psychological tests are systematically elevated due to the crisis of admission, there will be a tendency for during and post-treatment reductions to occur. It is therefore important to take account of this bias when making pre and post-treatment comparisons.

There are, of course, many other problems connected with establishing reliable and valid measures of the variables we are interested in, but I will not elaborate those now.

Interpretive Problems

In conclusion, I should like to draw attention to some problems which arise in trying to interpret the results we do obtain. Even when we are satisfied that the evidence in a study of a particular community suggests a causal relationship between treatment and improved outcome, we cannot infer that this would necessarily be repeated in the same community again, nor can we assume that other communities would achieve such results, nor can we assume that the population which has undergone treatment is in any way equivalent to the population of all drug abusers. The selection processes which operate either through personal choice on the part of the addict, or motivation tests on the part of the clinic staff, or inclusion criteria on the part of research workers, or a host of other more subtle factors, make it difficult to generalise from our conclusions. For this reason it is rare to find follow-up studies in the literature which can usefully be compared.

My subject has been problems in treatment evaluation and I hope that I have not wallowed in them too pessimistically since I have not felt obliged to provide any solutions. I will leave that difficult task to somebody else!

3

'Experiences in Groups'
Bion's Debt to Freud

In this chapter I am going to trace some links between Freud's thought and the ideas which Bion develops in the seven papers entitled 'Experiences in Groups'. although Bion emphasises the divergences between his own approach to the group and that of Freud, I am struck by the underlying similarities between Bion's approach to the group and Freud's approach to the individual.

In his introduction Bion observes that the psychoanalytic approach through the individual and his own approach through the group are dealing with different facets of the same phenomena. Bion sees the small-group setting as a new field of investigation with the potential to reveal hitherto obscure aspects of human nature. What he experiences in groups needs to be described and ordered, just as Freud needed to make sense of his experiences with individual patients. The essays, which are a mixture of clinical description and tentative theory-building, bring to mind Freud and Breuer's early 'Studies on Hysteria'. I think Bion applies to the group the same spirit of uncompromising introspective investigation that led Freud into the development of psychoanalysis. There is also evidence in these essays to show how the problems which preoccupy Bion are closely related in structure to those which preoccupied Freud. Similarly, Bion's theoretical solutions are patterned on the Freudian model.

Anna O. presented Freud and Breuer with a dramatic clinical picture in which two apparently contradictory and opposing states of mind existed in the same person. She was an intelligent, sympathetic young woman in one state somewhat melancholy and anxious, but relatively normal. In the other state, according to the case study, she hallucinated and was 'naughty', that is to say she was abusive, threw cushions at people, tore at her bedclothes and was stubbornly opposed to every therapeutic effort. At moments when her mind was clear she would complain of having two selves: a real one and an evil one which forced her to behave badly.

Freud, as we know, approached this problem with a topographical question. He asked himself where Anna's *condition seconde* came from and where it hid when not apparently present. We know that he then postulated a place, an

unconscious domain of the mind, in which unacceptable impulses were continuously seeking discharge and being held in check by a process of repression.

Now compare this with Bion's problem in his group. The group is composed
of intelligent and sympathetic people, eager and anxious to learn, yet it is
characterised by episodes of glumness and silence when members show little
interest in other's contributions and persistently complain about each other and
the atmosphere is heavy with apathy and fruitless effort. The one feeling
seemingly shared by all present is frustration. Bion thinks that the group is
somehow mentally united at a level which gives rise to this common feeling. He
asks himself:

> 'what is this group which is unsympathetic and hostile to our work? I must
> assume that it consists of these same people that I see struggling hard to
> do the work.' (p.48)

Again, he remarks:

> 'The picture of hard-working individuals striving to solve their
> psychological problems is displaced by a picture of a group mobilized to
> express its hostility and contempt for neurotic patients and for all who wish
> to approach neurotic problems seriously.' (p.48)

Bion has taken as his point of departure the observation of a paradoxical and
dramatic discontinuity in the mental life of the group and he has set himself the
task of describing and understanding it. Like Freud, he postulates a domain which
is to be the home of the group *condition seconde* and again like Freud he regards
it as a realm which cannot be directly observed but has to be inferred from the
behaviour of the group. It is of course the basic assumption group or group
mentality, which Bion then defines as:

> 'The unanimous expression of the will of the group, contributed to by the
> individual in ways of which he is unaware, influencing him disagreeably
> whenever he thinks or behaves in a manner at variance with the basic
> assumptions.' (p.65)

As far as the group is concerned, Bion tells us, the basic assumption is essentially
a tacit assumption. Individuals in a group behave *as if* they have adopted together
a shared common wish that they hope the group will fulfil. In Bion's developing
metapsychology of the group this common assumption arises as an integral part
of man's nature as a 'herd' animal and it seems to function according to the
'pleasure principle'. Thus, when group members begin to complain about their
treatment and wish for something better Bion comments:

> 'In the group it becomes very clear that this longed-for alternative to the
> group procedure is really something like arriving fully equipped as an adult
> fitted by instinct to know without training and development exactly how
> to live and move and have his being in a group.

There is only one kind of group and one kind of man that approximates to this dream, and that is the basic assumption group – the group dominated by one of the three basic assumptions, dependence, pairing and fight or flight – and the man who is able to sink his identity in the herd.' (p.89)

Later Bion elaborates his description of the basic assumption, saying:

'There is no direct conflict between basic assumptions but only changes from one state to another, which are either smooth transitions or brought about through intervention of the sophisticated group. They do not conflict, they alternate; conflict arises only at the junction between the basic group and the sophisticated group.' (p.96)

Compare this with Freud's famous description of the characteristics of the system *Ucs*:[1]

'The nucleus of the Ucs consists of instinctual representatives which seek to discharge their cathexis; that is to say it consists of wishful impulses. These instinctual impulses are co-ordinate with one another, exist side by side without being influenced by one another, and are exempt from mutual contradiction ...

There are in this system no negation, no doubt, no degrees of certainty: all this is only introduced by the work of the censorship between the Ucs and Pcs'. (*The Unconscious* 1915c, p.186)

It seems that Bion is constructing a topographical model for group psychology very much along the lines of Freud's early topography of the individual mind. The sophisticated or work group in Bion's system functions according to the 'reality principle'.[2] Here individuals retain their unique identity and are able consciously to cooperate to achieve a given end; the group has to deal with external reality and must therefore be logical and scientific. It is ranged against the basic assumption group in much the same way as Freud's system *Cs* conflicts with the system *Ucs*.

---

1   In his *Review of Group Dynamics* published later (in 1952) Bion emphasises timelessness as an important characteristic of basic assumption mentality, saying:
    'Time plays no part in it; it is a dimension of mental function that is not recognised; consequently all activities that require an awareness of time are imperfectly comprehended and tend to arouse feelings of persecution. Interpretations of activity on the level of the basic assumptions lay bare a disturbed relationship to time'. (p.158)
    This also accords with Freud's description of the system *Ucs*:
    'The processes of the system Ucs. are timeless; *i.e.* they are not ordered temporally; are not altered by the passage of time; they have no reference to time at all. Reference to time is bound up, once again, with the work of the system Cs.' (The Unconscious, p.187)
2   Bion makes this explicit in his 1952 review when he says of the work group:
    'Its characteristics are similar to those attributed by Freud (1911) to the ego'. (p.143)

According to Freud, in order to be complete, a metapsychological description of mental life should include three aspects: topographical, dynamic and economic. We must now examine Bion's psychology of the group in order to see whether he too has included the dynamic and economic aspects.

In Freud's system 'instincts' which arise biologically from a constant source of stimulation within the organism provide the dynamic forces which are then changed in different ways and somehow gain mental representation in the form of feelings and ideas. He is ambiguous in his use of the term but in 'Instincts and Their Vicissitudes' (1915a) he states that:

> '...an "instinct" appears to us as a concept on the frontier between the mental and the somatic, as the psychical representative of the stimuli originating from within the organism and reaching the mind, as a measure of the demand made upon the mind for work in consequence of its connection with the body'. (p.122)

The ambiguity as to whether the set of undifferentiated internal organic stimuli or the psychological representation should be called 'instinct' matters little; what is important is that Freud here is postulating two distinct levels of functioning which are somehow articulated with one another, although the leap from organic stimuli to psychic representation remains mysterious.

Consider Bion's approach to the group again. He postulates the existence of 'protomental phenomena', which are precursors to the emotions associated with the basic assumptions. Their relationship with the basic assumption groups is probably as mysterious as the relationship between Freud's instincts and their mental representatives but Bion says:

> 'The protomental system I visualise as one in which physical and psychological or mental are undifferentiated. It is a matrix from which spring the phenomena which at first appear – on a psychological level and in the light of psychological investigation – to be discrete feelings only loosely associated with one another. It is from this matrix that emotions proper to the basic assumption flow to reinforce, pervade, and, on occasion, to dominate the mental life of the group.' (p.102)

Bion, like Freud, has distinguished two levels of group mental life: an undifferentiated hidden level and a manifest level where symptoms may be expressed either physically or mentally or in combination.

Freudian psychology is predicated on the notion that there is inherent conflict between the instincts, so that simultaneous satisfaction of all instinctual desires is logically and actually impossible. Moreover, since they arise continuously from within the organism they cannot be avoided by a process of flight but have to be confronted in some way. Reality sets limits and imposes frustration upon the instinctual aims and it is for this reason that the mind has to do work in dealing with instinctual conflicts; it has to defend itself against their impossible demands.

The instincts therefore have to be modified by undergoing vicissitudes such as reversal, turning round upon the self, sublimation and repression. Freud puts it this way in his essay on Repression (1915b):

> 'We then learn that the satisfaction of an instinct which is under repression would be quite possible, and further, that in every instance such a satisfaction would be pleasurable in itself, but it would be irreconcilable with other claims and intentions. It would, therefore, cause pleasure in one place and unpleasure in another.' (p.147)

The essence of repression, Freud says, lies in simply turning something away so that it is kept at a distance from the conscious. Compare this now with Bion's view of the human dilemma:

> 'Various feelings, not in themselves unpleasant, indeed greatly desired by the individual, cannot be experienced except fixed in combination with other less desired and often strongly disliked feelings, so the individual has to resort to splitting to isolate himself from the group and from his own essential 'groupishness' – his inalienable quality as a herd animal.' (p.95)

The work group, whose job it is to deal with this conflict, is therefore confronted with the problem of resolving contradictory wishes in the basic assumptions seeking expression. The basic assumptions like Freud's instincts are therefore subject to different vicissitudes. They may be allowed to 'suffuse' the work group with their emotions; or as Bion puts it, the work group conspires with one particular assumption which it allows to develop at the expense of the others. On the other hand they may be confined to the level of the protomental phase, and this seems to be the group equivalent for Freud's process of repression in the individual.

I am suggesting therefore that in *Experiences in Groups* Bion has developed a metapsychology of groups which is equivalent in many respects to the system Freud devised as a model for the functioning of the individual human mind. Bion's group metapsychology has topographical, dynamic and (by implication) economic elements (that is, variations in the quantities of emotions). It pushes back the conflict between individual narcissism and the demands of group living into the essential nature of man as a 'herd animal'. It suggests that this conflict is dealt with by processes of splitting which are akin to the repressive mechanisms which Freud postulates.

4

On Helpful Homunculi

As the twentieth century draws to a close we can justifiably take pride in the progress of medical technology. Today we are able to produce wondrous images of the human brain using a variety of sophisticated computer aided techniques, and we have become used to seeing these brilliant coloured pictures as adjuncts to research and diagnosis. Pictures of the human mind are less frequently shown (though I propose to do so later in this chapter).

Nineteenth century romanticism, with its emphasis on an undefined order of things somehow transcending the everyday empirically observable world, was ushered out by modern science and the cult of the fact. Nowadays we are almost all Gradgrinds, reserving a sceptical and lofty contempt for anything fanciful. Yet we cannot escape from our own imaginations. The writings of the Romantic Poets are literary facts, just as our dreams are psychological facts – and if we ignore them, we turn away from our own nature as symbol making beings.

Not surprisingly, psychoanalysis, born a hundred years ago at the turn of the century, bears the stamp of both traditions. Freud tried all along to place it in the arena of empirical science and technology. Yet its concern with the 'invisible' world of the unconscious mind, and its emphasis on metaphor and meaning, make it more like one of the humanities.

Consider Melanie Klein's notion of an 'internal world' – a notion which is crucial to an understanding of her thought. We can take as our point of departure her 1940 paper 'Mourning and its relation to Manic-Depressive States'. I quote:

'Along with the child's relation, first to his mother and soon to his father and other people, go those processes of internalisation on which I have laid so much stress in my work. The baby, having incorporated his parents, feels them to be live people inside his body in the concrete way in which deep unconscious phantasies are experienced... They are in his mind, 'internal' or 'inner' objects, as I have termed them. Thus an inner world is being built up in the child's unconscious mind, corresponding to his actual experiences and the impressions he gains from people and the external world, and yet altered by his own phantasies and impulses. If it is a world of people predominantly at peace with each other and with the ego, inner harmony, security and integration ensue.' (pp.345–346)

I am not going to concern myself today with the justifications for this extraordinary statement about what a baby feels, but rather seek to understand what it might mean. What indeed is meant when Mrs Klein asserts that deep unconscious phantasies are experienced in a concrete way and that babies – or anyone else for that matter – feel their parents to be live people within their bodies!

In talking of deeply unconscious feelings there may appear to be a contradiction, for feelings are normally taken to be experiences of which we are conscious. How then can we have a feeling and yet be unaware that we are having it? There is nothing specifically 'Kleinian' about this problem, of course, for in talking this way Mrs. Klein was simply following in a well trodden psychoanalytic tradition. The legitimacy of the expression 'unconscious sense of guilt' together with all its analogues – 'unconscious hatred', 'unconscious envy', 'unconscious lust', 'unconscious ideas' and so forth had indeed been called into question by Freud in his early essay on 'The Unconscious' (1915c); and one can do no better now than to restate that these unconscious experiences have to be inferred from the data of consciousness, because by definition they are not directly available to observation or introspection. As Klein (1936) put it in another paper:

> 'I do not mean that the 'internalised' good parents will consciously be felt as such (even in the small child the feeling of possessing them inside is deeply unconscious). They are not felt consciously to be there, but rather as something within the personality having the nature of kindness and wisdom; this leads to confidence and trust in oneself and helps to combat and overcome the feelings of fear of having bad figures within one and of being governed by one's own uncontrollable hatred, and furthermore, this leads to trust in people in the outside world beyond the family circle.' (p.295)

Let us compare these passages from Melanie Klein to what Freud has to say about the 'Internal World' in his *Outline of Psychoanalysis* (1940). Here he presents us with a picture of childhood development in which up to the age of about five years the child has only to reconcile the satisfaction of instinctual needs with the constraints of external reality. At this age, however, he suggests that an important change in the structure of the child's mind occurs:

> 'A portion of the external world has, at least partially, been abandoned as an object and has instead, by identification, been taken into the ego and thus become an integral part of the internal world. This new psychical agency continues to carry on the functions which have hitherto been performed by the people [the abandoned objects] in the external world: it observes the ego, gives it orders, judges it and threatens it with punishments, exactly like the parents whose place it has taken. We call this agency the SUPER-EGO and are aware of it in its judicial functions as our CONSCIENCE. It is a remarkable thing that the super-ego often displays

severity for which no model has been provided by the real parents...'
(p.205)

A severity which Freud goes on to say:

'...corresponds to the strength of the defence used against the temptation
of the Oedipus complex.' (p.206)

Both Freud and Klein therefore agree that the characteristics of the real parents
(distorted by the child's own desires, prohibitions and phantasies) are incorporated into the mind and remain there as distinct entities, marked off from the
subjective sense of self. Freud tends to hypostatise this by talking of a 'psychic
agency', whereas Klein tends to anthropomorphise by talking of 'live people'
within the child's body. Nevertheless we must remember that Klein is trying to
reconstruct the individual's experiences as seen from within, whereas Freud is
looking from without in an attempt at schematic organisation. Timing aside
therefore, I think there is a good measure of agreement in principle between the
two.

If by definition we can have no direct knowledge of internal reality, but must
be satisfied with transformations manifested in the conscious mind, where then
should we look in the perceived world of common sense for evidence of this
inner underlying world which Freud invests us with and which Klein is describing? What external manifestations will help us most easily to grasp the inner
happenings?

It is common knowledge that Freud regarded dreams as the Royal Road to
the Unconscious, as well as slips of the tongue, jokes, fairy tales, linguistic usage
and other cultural artifacts. A broad sweep of all these sources reveals that there
is nothing unfamiliar in the idea that a person may believe his body to be
inhabited by other beings than himself. It is a commonplace in medieval
demonology, in anthropology, and in a multi-cultural society such as our own,
in the every day practice of general psychiatry.

We must also take into account religious experiences of a transcendental nature
and the notion of 'soul'. Gerard Manley Hopkins (1970) communicates his
tremendous sense of having been penetrated and totally infused by his deity when
he says:

'Thou hast bound bones and veins in me, fastened me flesh/And after it
almost unmade, what with dread/Thy doing: and dost thou touch me
afresh?/ Over again I feel thy finger and find thee.' (p.51)

The experience of being inhabited by a non-corporeal element which determines
one's feelings or actions is clearly part of the human condition, brought into
being perhaps by the early experience of sensations and ideas for which we can
find no external referent. The idea that this inner figure can be helpful is also
appealing. What, for example, are we to make of the widespread appeal of
Grimm's well known tale 'The Shoemaker and the Elves' (Owens 1981). In this

tale a shoemaker, through no fault of his own, becomes so poor that he is down to his last piece of leather. He cuts the leather and lays it on his bench in readiness to begin work the following morning. When he awakes however, he finds the shoes already made and beautifully stitched. He is rescued from poverty by mysterious forces which work on his behalf. One night gratitude leads him to want to find out who is helping him. He decides to sit up and watch. As the clock strikes twelve, two pretty little elves, without a morsel of clothes to cover them seat themselves at his work-bench and labour furiously throughout the night. He and his wife provide the elves with clothes in order to repay their kindness.

Does this fairy tale express a deep psychological truth? In fact, because artists and writers are primarily concerned with giving concrete expression in the outer world to inchoate inner experiences, it is precisely in their work that the nature of the inner world is most likely to be revealed. Religious works aside, the world of art remains replete with examples of the artist experiencing himself as subordinate to an inner object. Not only may this 'inner object' inspire composition but the artist or composer may come to rely on it to such an extent that he feels himself to be a mere copyist or secretary, taking dictation from his internal object. The ease with which Mozart, Schubert, Beethoven, Liszt and others are alleged to have composed and extemporised is consistent with this view of things as is the vision of the inspirational poets as being 'servants to their muse'. William Blake, for example, believed that his words were often dictated to him by some super-natural power (Bowra 1961, p.43).

And who do you think was the true author of *Dr. Jekyll and Mr. Hyde?* According to Robert Louis Stevenson (1913), the book was written by helpful little people. '...they are just my Brownies, God bless them' he says,

'...who do one half my work for me while I am fast asleep, and in all human likelihood, do the rest for me as well, when I am wide awake and fondly suppose I do it for myself. That part which is done while I am sleeping is the Brownies' part beyond contention; but that which is done when I am up and about is by no means necessarily mine, since all goes to show the Brownies have a hand in it even then. Here is a doubt that much concerns my conscience. For myself – what I call I, my conscious ego, the denizen of the pineal gland unless he has changed his residence since Descartes, the man with the conscience and the variable bank account, the man with the hat and the boots, and the privilege of voting and not carrying his candidate at the general elections – I am sometimes tempted to suppose he is no story-teller at all, but a creature as matter of fact as any cheesemonger or any cheese, and a realist bemired up to the ears in actuality, so that, by that account, the whole of my published fiction should be the single-handed product of some Brownie, some Familiar, some unseen collaborator, whom I keep locked in a back garret, while I get all the praise,

and he but a share (which I cannot prevent him getting) of the pudding.'
(p.165)

Interestingly, Freud too, clearly felt indebted to a little man. In 1895, writing to
his friend Wilhelm Fliess about his inability to give up smoking, he says:

'I began it again because I constantly missed it (after fourteen months
abstinence) and because I must treat this psychic fellow well or he won't
work for me. I demand a great deal of him. The torment, most of the time,
is superhuman.' (Freud 1985)

It is no coincidence that the exploration of the twilight area of unconscious
phantasy in poetry is often linked with a state of confusion. The poet doubts his
own judgement and is unable to assess his level of consciousness. Keats' (Keats
1906) famous ending to his 'Ode to a Nightingale' illustrates this:

'Was it a vision or a waking dream?
Fled is that music; – do I wake or sleep?'

and we can see it again in the work of the Victorian poet Arthur Hugh Clough
(Norrington 1968) (Dipsychus Scene XII)

'I had a vision; was it in my sleep?
And if it were what then? But sleep or wake,
I saw a great light open oe'r my head;
And sleep or wake, uplifted to that light,
Out of that light proceeding heard a voice
Uttering high words, which, whether sleep or wake,
In me were fixed, and in me must abide.

"When the enemy is near thee
Call on us!
In our hands we will upbear thee,
We shall neither scathe nor scare thee,
Call on us."'

George Eliot, in her last novel *Daniel Deronda*, gives us a more explicit picture of
a helpful 'internal mother'. She is describing the grief of a young woman Mirah,
who believes her mother to be dead.

'I used to cry every night in my bed for a long while. Then when she came
so often to me in my sleep, I thought she must be living about me though
I could not always see her, and that comforted me. I was never afraid in
the dark because of that; and very often in the day I used to shut my eyes
and bury my face and try to see her and to hear her singing. I came to do
that at last without shutting my eyes.' (p.252)

The point which needs to be emphasised here once again is the way that the
internal mother is experienced as autonomous – leading a life of her own. It is
this aspect of Melanie Klein's statement, the contention that the inner world of

the mind *is experienced* as being peopled by independent characters *with a life of their own* which lies at the heart of her work; and it is the way in which the happenings in this interior world inform the events of everyday life and are the prime determinants of our experience, mood and behaviour, which concern her.

But it was not an appreciation of art or a reading of literature which was the main stimulus to her ideas; it was of course the observation of children at play in her consulting room. Here Klein conceived a laboratory for the investigation of interior happenings represented and exteriorised in the imaginative play of her small patients, and it was here that the evidence for her view of the mind was gathered. Anyone who comes into contact with children can observe further examples for themselves, which are consistent with the notion that internal parents are experienced as existing independently.

I was once treating a five-year-old girl who had presented with various symptoms associated with school refusal. On her fourth session her mother decided to wait in the corridor immediately opposite the door to my consulting room, and not in the main reception area of the clinic. The child came bounding into the room, rushed over to the toys and started playing enthusiastically saying, 'I like these cars'. Then she went back to the door, telling her mother rather officiously to go and sit in the reception area. Having done this she returned to the toys and turning the cars upside down to make them into boats, she proceeded to put a mummy and daddy into one boat and a little boy and little girl figure into another. Suddenly she bashed the two boats together with great force, knocking the mummy and daddy overboard!

Almost immediately she became acutely anxious and began asking for her mother. I responded by suggesting that like the blue boat, she felt she had been naughty and that she was afraid that she would lose her mother because she had told her to go away into the reception area and preferred to play with me. At this point she embraced me in tears and began to draw a picture of her mother, but stopped half way and ran to the door again. I told her that I would take her back to mother when we had finished and she nodded in agreement, but then it was I who was taken aback to hear a kind of low pitched grown up voice emanate from her, whispered under her breath, it said: 'Don't worry. It'll be alright, love.'

I think this vignette illustrates graphically the interplay between internal and external world phenomena. We can infer that the attack on the toy parents (which may have gone further than originally intended) represented an attack on phantasised parents whom she confidently thought she could do without, while she enjoyed herself playing with me. But it is clear that no sooner had the damage been done in phantasy to her internal mother, than she became overwhelmed with anxiety about losing her real mother waiting in reception. An attempt was then made to reconstruct her picture of mother, and when this failed, anxiety was temporarily alleviated by a reassuring maternal voice from within.

She was unable to continue playing during the rest of the session, telling me that she felt 'sad in her body' and sitting anxiously watching the clock. When she heard the noise of a train in the distance she worried that her mother would be on it and when she heard an ice-cream van outside she said it was playing a lullaby. 'If she's out in the snow I'll be very sad,' she said reflectively, and then 'I'm worried that she's angry with me and gone without me because I've been naughty, but I haven't really' Then she added, 'I like the snow and hate rain. You can play with snow.'

Once again we may note how she experienced her sadness as a concrete bodily sensation, how it inhibited her capacity to play, and how she struggled with the separation anxiety, making use of external chance happenings and sounds, filling them with personal meaning, summoning up a helpful inner being, in a moving and courageous struggle to deal with her inner conflict.

A nine-year-old boy produced the advent calendar shown in Figure 1 for his mother which can be taken as an amusing representation of his inner world. The various different guises in which his mother appears to him may be represented by Miss World, the Queen and, looming large, the slinky figure in the centre. But look what happens when we open up the doors in her body (Figure 2)!

The little boy with the dog in the bottom right hand corner probably represents the child himself (the door number is nine). There is a frog in the genital area, three balloons in the abdomen, perhaps his phantasised siblings inside mummy's tummy, a delicious red-nosed reindeer breast and nipple on one side, and a forbidding cold snowman breast on the other. Her functions may include the provision of food and the giving of toys, but also perhaps the 'zoom, crash, patter' attached to her hand brings to mind the administration of punishment. Her face is a loveable soft furry pet mouse with big eyes, and looking down on it all a bright star (top left), and John Lennon with his dark glasses in the top right hand corner, representing perhaps his father above him, turning a blind eye to his oedipal desires!

All this may seem fanciful and arbitrary, but to my mind it provides a graphic representation of the complex unconscious world of inner phantasy, populated with multi-layered, Russian doll-like figures. Susan Isaac's early paper (1952) on 'The nature and Function of Phantasy' remains the best exposition of the Kleinian view and is worth looking at in some detail, particularly in order to understand the putative biological link between unconscious phantasy and the instincts – the contribution to internal objects which, so to speak, comes from within and ensures that they are not just carbon copies of their external counterparts.

As early as 1915 in his paper on *Instincts and their Vicissitudes*, Freud (1915a) linked the experience of instinctual stimuli with the generation of an internal world. 'Let us imagine ourselves in the situation of an almost entirely helpless living organism, as yet unoriented in the world,' he said.

Figure 1

Figure 2

'This organism will very soon be in a position to make a first distinction and a first orientation. On the one hand it will be aware of stimuli which can be avoided by muscular action (flight); these it ascribes to an external world. On the other hand it will also be aware of stimuli against which such action is of no avail and whose character of constant pressure persists in spite of it; these stimuli are signs of an internal world, the evidence of instinctual needs. The perceptual substance of the living organism will thus have found in the efficacy of its muscular activity a basis for distinguishing between an "outside" and an "inside".' (p.119)

Picking up Freud's notion that somatic impulses (instincts) have to be represented in the mind (both conscious and unconscious) by *ideas*, Isaacs suggests that these ideas, organised into complex patterns are precisely what is meant by the term 'unconscious phantasy', and are the building materials of the internal world. More than this, she suggests that it is not only instincts which have to be represented thus, but also the means developed for inhibiting and controlling those instincts, namely defence mechanisms such as denial, reassurance, omnipotent control, reparation etc. These processes too must all be represented by ideas in unconscious phantasy, and it is the interplay between them that gives rise to mental life. The world of phantasy, she says:

'...shows the same protean and kaleidoscopic changes as the contents of a dream. These changes occur partly in response to external stimulation and partly as a result of the interplay between the primary instinctual urges themselves.' (p.84)

A telling example is quoted from the analysis of a small girl. This girl as a baby had shown no interest whatsoever in feeding; she had refused to suck her mother's breast from birth, and had continued to eat very little and never without persuasion. It soon became clear from her play that she was continually biting. 'Among other things, she pretended to be a biting dog, a crocodile, a lion, a pair of scissors, a mincing machine and a machine for grinding cement.' It is inferred that the bodily pangs of hunger were experienced by this baby as fearful bites liable to hurt herself or her mother when she fed. Failure to feed would have led to an increase in hunger, thus setting up a vicious circle.

Because the earliest phantasies are built on bodily experiences, at first scarcely capable of being related to an external object, they acquire the quality of 'me-ness', and are experienced physically. Visual perceptions too, originating from external light stimuli, may at first be experienced as coming from within. Gradually, however, they become distinguished as images of independent objects in the external world and it is realised as Isaacs put it:

'that the objects are outside the mind, but their images are "in the mind".' (p.105)

The power of these images, to affect feelings, behaviour, character and personality in later life, remains rooted in their repressed unconscious somatic associates — in the unconscious world of emotion and desire.

We have come a long way with Isaacs, but if we leave the story here we will have missed out the most important bit! When we think merely of the psychical representations of instincts and defences we are thinking mechanically. But if we think twice, we will realise that it is exactly in the process of imbuing biological impulses with psychological significance that symbols and meaning are generated. This process remains mysterious and infinitely diverse. We do not understand how impulses are transmuted into symbols, and this remains as true for Freud's superego as it does for Klein's internal parents.

How are symbols formed? And what can we say about the transactions which produce differences in the quality and value between them? These are the predominant questions that underlie the Kleinian enquiry and according to Donald Meltzer give an entirely new significance to the concept of phantasy and the way we look at dreams. After Melanie Klein, Meltzer (1984) says:

'Dreaming could not be viewed merely as a process for allaying tensions in order to maintain sleep; dreams had to be seen as pictures of dream life that was going on all the time, awake or asleep. We may call these transactions 'dreams' when we are asleep, and 'unconscious phantasies' when we are awake. The implication was that this internal world must be assigned the full significance of a place, a life-space, perhaps the place where meaning was generated. Freud's formulation of the super-ego could be expanded and transformed into the concept of internal objects. Psychic reality could be treated in a concrete way as a place where relationships were taking place and where the meaning of life was generated for deployment to the outside world.' (p.38)

5

Some Implications of Melanie Klein's Thought for Clinical Practice

In this chapter I want to think about some of the implications of Melanie Klein's thought for clinical practice. To be rational our clinical practice must be based on a model of the mind which we hold to, and a method of bringing about change which we adopt. Melanie Klein inherited Freud's structural model, together with the psychoanalytical method based on free association. But as we have seen, with her notion of unconscious phantasy she transformed the model, and with her innovations in play technique she was able to discover and explore previously uncharted territory. This in turn had profound implications for the practice of adult psychoanalysis.

The material which the patient was asked to bring to the session —namely free associations, dreams, and observable behaviour, remained of course the same; but the unconscious meaning which the analyst was able to infer, using Klein's conceptual framework was radically and qualitatively different. Furthermore the interplay between the analyst's interpretive activity and the dynamics of the patient's internal world gave rise to a new and more precise therapeutic process. This meant that the analyst was not only required to pay attention to new details in the patient's material but also as Klein put it: '…to deal with the changes in content and form which anxiety situations undergo with every new insight achieved.'

In 1905 Freud had been able to express the therapeutic aim of psychoanalysis quite simply – to make what was unconscious conscious, and this was in keeping with the topographical model which he had put forward based on his Studies on Hysteria. Eighteen years later in his most sophisticated formulation, he saw the work of analysis more in terms of 'strengthening the ego' in its constant battle to reconcile the demands of its 'three tyrannical masters' – the id, the superego and the external world (Freud 1923).

On this view, unpleasant experiences known as anxiety, are produced when the ego fails in its task. If the ego is obliged to admit its weakness, Freud (1932) said,

'...it breaks out in anxiety – realistic anxiety regarding the external world, moral anxiety regarding the superego and neurotic anxiety regarding the strength of the passions in the id.' (p.78)

But on the other hand, one must assume that if the ego is strong, and succeeds in its task, it will willingly tolerate and acknowledge the passions of the id, even when they are unsatisfied and unrequited, and will equally tolerate the strictures of the superego, however punitive or guilt provoking – and all this without deforming its perception of reality. This, of course, is recogniseable as a picture not unlike Melanie Klein's 'depressive position'.

So the end points, the notion of a strong and integrated ego, an adult ego or an ego which has reached the 'depressive position' in Klein's language, may not be so different as prototypes of mental health —but how does analysis in the Kleinian tradition help a person to achieve this? How in other words does it facilitate the development from 'paranoid-schizoid' to 'depressive' position?

Let us start by looking at what Melanie Klein (1961) had to say about this in her concluding remarks to the *Narrative of a Child Analysis*

'I achieved this (the diminution of persecutory anxieties) by again and again analyzing anxieties relating to his internal objects and his destructive impulses. From another angle Richard's progress was bound up with improvement in his relation to his good object; and it is my conviction that this is fundamentally the case in every analysis in which we can bring about some lasting favourable alterations.' (p.465)

She goes on to explain that this young boy's relation to both mother and analyst had been based on idealisation, which she says is always necessarily linked with persecution in various degrees. It may not be apparent at first sight why this should be so. I think the explanation is as follows: idealisation is a defensive distortion of reality which is always multifaceted. It is an attempt to deny unacceptable, painful, frightening or guilt-provoking aspects of an object, which are detached from it or split off and psychologically 'got rid of'. The object then appears to be faultless, but this is achieved at the expense of the truth, and moreover the unwanted aspects have to 'go somewhere'. Every idealised relationship must therefore be accompanied by a reciprocal persecutory relationship which has been denied, and it is the existence of this in the unconscious mind which is the root of many symptoms.

The gradual lessening of this split, it seems, is facilitated in analysis by the recognition and acknowledgement of persecutory anxiety and its connection to the individual's own destructive impulses. Again why should this be so? Surely you will argue, it can do nothing but harm to remind a distressed person of their own destructiveness! This is indeed the case if such interpretations are carried out in an unskilful way, or in a situation where the analyst is unable to deal with or modulate the patient's suffering. Under these circumstances the result is likely to be an increase in defensive splitting, regression to the paranoid-schizoid position, and the possible development of a full blown picture of what psychiatrists call 'depressive illness'. When, however, it proves possible to help the patient come to terms with the split-off destructive impulses, a most amazing thing tends to take place. The reparative drive is stimulated, and this gives rise to all sorts of constructive activity and an increased ability to tolerate faults and deficiencies which previously would have been experienced as persecutory.

The patient's internal object is converted from a fragile idealised cipher, into a strong and 'good' object, or in other words, an object whose faults have been forgiven. This distinction is crucial, an idealised object is not a good object; a good object is an integrated object whose frustrating qualities are willingly borne, and it is the introjection of such an object into the structure of the ego which so strengthens its capacity to love, and sense of security and well-being.

We can easily follow these processes in clinical situations, but first I want to flesh out what I've been saying by reference to a literary example. I want to consider Shakespeare's play *The Winter's Tale*.

In this play we see the king, Leontes, inexplicably turn against his pregnant wife, Hermione, and accuse her of adultery with his best friend Polixenes. When she eventually gives birth to a baby girl, he casts the child out and sentences his wife to death. His jealousy appears totally without foundation or even provocation (for there is no Iago in this play). It is an act of mad, outrageous destructiveness toward his faithful, loving and good wife. We can only infer that it is the pregnancy itself which has 'faulted' Hermione, and turned her from an idealised object in Leontes eyes, into an object of contempt and hatred.

> '...let her sport herself
> With that she's big with; for tis Polixenes
> Has made thee swell thus.' (*The Winters Tale* II.1.60)

he says.

Now if we saw this as a report on internal events in our patient, we would have to interpret Leontes' destructiveness, and risk him throwing another tantrum. But this is precisely what the Delphic oracle does in the play. When consulted as to Hermione's guilt, the oracle responds:

> 'Hermione is chaste; Polixenes
> blameless; Camillo a true subject;
> Leontes a jealous tyrant; his innocent babe truly begotten
> and the king shall live without an heir, if that
> which is lost be not found.' (*The Winters Tale* III.2.134)

By this time the damage has of course been done, his small son Camillus has already died of a broken heart through worry over his mother, and Hermione herself, when she hears the news, also swoons and dies. Leontes is desolate, he has lost everything. His internal world has collapsed, his objects are dead, and he and his own insane jealousy are responsible for the whole disaster.

These events and the oracle's words, however, seem to set in motion a change in the King's state of mind; he is no longer the omnipotent tyrant, but rather recognising his own culpability, he is becoming a remorseful penitent. 'Prithee, bring me to the dead bodies of my queen and son', he says, and:

> 'One grave shall be for both: upon them shall
> the causes of their death appear, unto
> Our shame perpetual. Once a day I'll visit
> The chapel where they lie, and tears shed there…
>
> Shall be my recreation: so long as nature
> Will bear up with this exercise, so long
> I daily vow to use it. Come and lead me
> Unto these sorrows.' (*The Winter's Tale* III.2.236)

In fact, Shakespeare makes Leontes (with the help of Paulina) grieve for sixteen years, before Hermione, in the form of a statue, is miraculously brought back to life and steps off her plinth. 'O, she's warm', Leontes exclaims, and we may infer that his interior world has been reconstructed and imbued with life once again.

> 'If this be magic, let it be an art
> Lawful as eating.'[1] (*The Winter's Tale* V.3.110)

he says, and we could perhaps hope the same for the practice of psychoanalytical psychotherapy.

Let us now turn to an example from clinical practice that bears an extraordinary resemblance to the preceding tale. It illustrates once again the way that an internal object can be brought back to life, through the creative process of mourning – a process which the author here links with the unconscious phantasy of orally incorporating the lost object. Had Shakespeare sensed the connection?

This example comes from Karl Abraham, Klein's second analyst and mentor, and is described in his (1924b) 'Short Study of the Development of the Libido'. We should bear in mind that this work both antedated and informed Klein's later conceptual development.

Abraham had a patient whose wife was pregnant, but died tragically during a caesarian section, together with her prematurely born baby. Some time afterwards the husband resumed his analysis and reported that following his wife's death, he had been unable to eat for several weeks. One day, however, his appetite returned and he ate a good meal in the evening. The same night he dreamt that he was present at the post-mortem of his late wife. The dream was divided into two contrasting scenes. In one, the separate parts of her body grew together again, the dead woman began to show life, and he embraced her with

---

1   The connection with oral incorporation in following example!

feelings of the liveliest joy. In the other the dissecting room altered its appearance, and the dreamer was reminded of slaughtered animals in a butcher's shop.

The dreamer's association to this dream, brought out the remarkable fact, Abraham tells us, that the sight of his wife's dissected body reminded him of his meal, and especially of a meat dish he had eaten the night before. Abraham (1924b) comments:

> 'Consuming the flesh of the dead wife is made equivalent to restoring her to life...the widowed man had abandoned himself to his grief for a certain period of time as though there were no possible escape from it. His disinclination for food was in part a playing with his own death; it seemed to imply that now that the object of his love was dead, life had no more attraction for him. He then began to work off the traumatic effect of his loss by means of an unconscious process of introjection of the loved object. While this was going on he was once more able to take nourishment, and at the same time his dream announced the fact that the work of mourning had succeeded.' (pp.435–436)

The idea of 'introjective identification', something which Freud touched on in his famous essay on 'Mourning and Melancholia' (1917, p.239) when he talked about the '...shadow of the lost object falling upon the ego', and again in his understanding of the 'dissolution of the oedipus complex' and the creation of the superego, can be seen to reach its zenith in the work of Melanie Klein. It is this process – the introjection of a good breast and its incorporation into the structure of the ego which is understood to lay the basis for mental health. The psychoanalytic process then becomes a means of removing blocks to this development and helping to foster it. How does the analyst come to be able to play a part in such an important personal process? In order to understand this we must briefly consider the concept of 'transference' and the changes in its meaning implied by the Kleinian perspective.

As is well known Freud first saw transference as an obstacle to psychoanalytic progress but later came to reconceptualise it as the central tool of the analyst. In the 'Question of Lay Analysis' published in 1926, he gives a nice account of transference, describing it as a kind of compulsive love which disregards every variation in personal attraction, age, sex, or class. He goes on:

> 'In proportion as the purely sensual and the hostile sides of his love try to show themselves, the patient's opposition to them is aroused. He struggles against them and tries to repress them before our very eyes. And now we understand what is happening. The patient is repeating in the form of falling in love with the analyst mental experiences which he has already been through once before; he has transferred on to the analyst mental attitudes that are lying ready in him and were intimately connected with his neurosis. He is also repeating before our eyes his old defensive actions; he would like best to repeat in his relation to the analyst all the history of

that forgotten period of his life. So what he is showing us is the kernel of his intimate life history: *he is reproducing it tangibly as though it were actually happening instead of remembering it*. In this way the riddle of transference love is solved and the analysis can proceed on its way – with the *help* of the new situation which had seemed such a menace to it.' [italic original] (p.226)

Now there are two aspects of this formulation to which I want to draw your attention. First, Freud says that the patient would like to repeat *all* the history of the forgotten period of his life. But what is this *all*? Clearly it is going to depend on what we imagine might have gone on during this forgotten period, and here Melanie Klein's hypotheses added a whole new dimension.

In her (1952) paper on the 'Origins of Transference', she outlines these ideas, which I will not reiterate now, and then states:

> I hold that transference originates in the same processes which in the earliest stages determine object-relations. Therefore we have to go back again and again in analysis to the fluctuations between objects, loved and hated, external and internal, which dominate early infancy. We can fully appreciate the interconnection between positive and negative transferences *only if we explore the early interplay between love and hate and the vicious circle of aggression, anxieties, feelings of guilt and increased aggression*, as well as the various aspects of objects towards whom these conflicting emotions and anxieties are directed.[my italics] (p.53)

Returning now to the quotation from Freud we remember he said that the transference tangibly reproduces this early life history *as though* it were actually happening. Now Klein's vision of 'internal reality' casts this 'as though' in a different light, for we have already discussed the concreteness with which she endowed internal figures. Therefore, for Klein there is no 'as though'. The events in the internal world are happening, and they are happening in the mind of the analysand over and over again. The infantile object-relations are not just part of history, they are re-enacted every day and manifest themselves in the heat of the analytical moment, in the here and now of the transference, where they can be recognised and interpreted by anyone who has eyes to see!

Donald Meltzer (1984) puts it well when he says:

> 'Instead of transference phenomena being seen as relics of the past they could now be viewed as externalisations of the immediate present of the internal situation, to be studied as psychic reality. Neurotics would not be seen as 'suffering from reminiscences' but could be thought of as *living in the past*, represented in the immediate present qualities of the internal world.' (p.39)

One more example, this time from my own practice, will serve to illustrate the way that inner happenings can be seen, and incidentally, that cannibalistic phantasies did not stop with Abraham's work in the 1920s but are still alive and well!

The patient in question was in five times weekly analysis. During the beginning of her fourth week she came to a consultation feeling an inexplicable sense of fear – she could not say what she was afraid of, and mentioned several events in her life which might have been relevant. Amongst these were a forthcoming examination, and having to move her room which involved separating from a female flat-mate of whom she was fond. Her boy-friend too was moving, and all this seemed important at a common-sense level, but it did not satisfy her as a sufficient understanding of her state of mind.

She went on to report some dream fragments. In one dream *her teeth were coming out*; that is all she could remember. But then came a second dream which she reported with an embarrassed giggle: *She was with a group of other girls in a supermarket, cutting up babies and packaging them and then giving them to their mothers to eat. The only trouble was, she added, that they had difficulty in doing up the polythene packages, because the babies wouldn't stop bleeding.* She went on to tell me that in childhood she had always been worried that an intruder would come up the stairs, and that as a result she had insisted that her mother slept with her at night.

In this little cameo we have a picture of her inner life which fills her inexplicable sense of anxiety with deeper meaning. In the first dream fragment she seems to be disarming herself by losing her teeth, clearly it is not going to be her that eats any babies! (In point of fact she was a vegetarian.) But this gives way in the second dream, with the encouragement of the mindless group (her so called friends) to a bloodthirsty and grotesque attack upon 'mummy's babies'. Furthermore it seems that the responsibility for this attack was wont to be transferred onto the phantasised intruder, who probably also represented her father. Her own identification with the intruder, however, was confirmed in the transference situation, when she noticed her reluctance to ring twice on the front door bell of my consulting room. She said it was like going into a shop where the shopkeeper did not want her to go in, as he thought she might be stealing something. Her parents had in fact owned a small shop in which she was brought up.

In this example we can see clearly the link between the destructive impulses of the patient and the paranoid anxiety which they generated. We can see the attempts in phantasy to transform the anxiety situation and shift the responsibility, and the need for reassurance from mother (manifested in the sleeping arrangements) that the babies were in fact safe and undamaged.

Of course there are other stories that one could tell about this material, and this one makes no claim to be either authoritative or comprehensive, even within the Kleinian tradition of analysis. It does nevertheless give some indication of the kind of imaginative thinking involved in this approach.

6

The Cradle of Violence
Reflections on the Perversion of Meaning

I want briefly to sketch out a psychological approach to the subject of violence. We find it easy to recognise violent and aggressive behaviour when it occurs. Behaviour is empirically observable and there is something quite unequivocal about the destruction of a material object: if physical injury is inflicted upon a person or damage done to property, we are rarely in any doubt about the nature of the act which we have witnessed.

Violence, however, can be understood in another sense, which the dictionary describes as 'weakened' but I would suggest may be more fundamental; namely the perversion of meaning. Indeed it seems to me likely that an act of violence in this sense may be a necessary antecedent to all violent behaviour.

Let me try to elaborate this idea. I am proposing that some form of psychological violence, something essentially located within a person's interior world, precedes, informs, and occurs *pari passu* with violent action. This perversion of meaning that is the cradle of violent behaviour is by its very nature unavailable for examination to the casual external observer; for from the outside we cannot normally see subtle alterations in the symbolic value accorded to the contents of another person's imagination. Such processes are essentially private, and we are dependent on consent, co-operation, and accurate introspective reporting if we are to build up a picture of someone else's inner life.

But there *is* a public forum, perhaps a marketplace, where people can display symbols, infuse them with meaning, negotiate their connotive value and generally deal in the commerce of semantics – I refer of course to language itself.

When an attempt is made grossly to pervert meaning in the public sphere, to coerce a change or devaluation of our shared symbols, we generally call it *propaganda* which we warn ourselves to beware. We consider that our intelligence has been subject to a violent insult.

Just how political language comes to consist largely of euphemism, question-begging, and sheer cloudy vagueness in order to name things without calling up a mental picture of their true horror is demonstrated by George Orwell in his *Politics and the English Language* (1946):

'Defenceless villages are bombarded from the air, the inhabitants driven out into the countryside, the cattle machine-gunned, the huts set on fire with incendiary bullets: this is called *pacification*. Millions of peasants are robbed of their farms and sent trudging down the road with no more than they can carry: this is called *transfer of population* or *rectification of frontiers*. People are imprisoned for years without trial, or shot in the back of the neck or set to die of scurvy in Arctic lumber camps, this is called *elimination of unreliable elements*.' [italics original] (p.153)

Nowadays we have become so used to this that we take it for granted even in domestic politics, and in wartime we inevitably expect to be bombarded not only with bombs and missiles, but also with dissonant meanings. Furthermore we recognise that we ourselves actively engage in linguistic distortions in order to legitimise our own violence. In the language of the military communiqué, the diversity and uniqueness of many individuals are transformed into a single composite threatening object know as 'the enemy'; targets rather than people are hit; and the dirty work of killing people becomes transformed into the sanitary work of a 'mopping-up', 'flushing-out', or 'cleaning-up' operation.

These are not metaphors we are dealing with but true violations of meaning, just as Himmler was not speaking metaphorically when referring to the effect of the destruction of five million European Jews on the German people. In 1943 he said:

'We don't want in the end, just because we have exterminated a germ, to be infected by that germ and die from it ... but on the whole we can say that we have fulfilled this heavy task with love for our people and we have not been damaged in the innermost of our being, our soul, our character.' (Hilberg 1961, p.642)

Preoccupation with admiration of the Nazis together with an addiction to the writings of the Marquis de Sade is of course not infrequently found in the most vicious of criminal murderers. Ian Brady, the Moors murderer, studied German in order to be able to read *Mein Kampf* in the original, while his young disciple David Smith wrote in his diary:

'Rape is not a crime, it is a state of mind. Murder is a hobby and a supreme pleasure. God is a superstition, a cancer that eats into the brain. People are like maggots, small, blind and worthless.' (Wilson 1984)

Clearly the common thread here lies in the insistence that the value of human life should be reduced to that accorded to invertebrates and microscopic organisms – an idea with which de Sade himself was obsessed. The keystone of this philosophy lies in the denial of psychic reality and the assertion that we live in a meaningless universe. By insisting that the random events of nature in the external world are the only reality, an attack of immense proportion is mounted upon the internal world of meaning and value: witness the following passage from de Sade's *The New Justine*:

> 'Now all forms are equal in the eyes of nature; nothing is lost in the gigantic cauldron in which her variations are produced: every piece of matter that falls into it instantly springs forth in other guises. *And of what significance is it to her creative hand* if this piece of flesh, which today conforms to the shape of a two-legged creature, is tomorrow brought forth as a thousand different insects?' [my italics] (Sade 1966)

As Janine Chasseguet-Smirgel (1985) has pointed out in her lucid and penetrating essay '*Perversion and the Universal Law*', de Sade's 'philosophical' arguments reveal but one basic intention: to reduce the universe to faeces, or rather to annihilate the universe of difference (the genital universe) and put in its place the anal universe in which all particles are equal and interchangeable. She makes it easy for us to see how such a manoeuvre assuages mental pain, for by abolishing all sense of difference, feelings of inadequacy, castration, loss, absence and death are at the same time rendered non-existent.

But if we can see the perversion of meaning writ large in the Sadeian imagination and translated into action in the social arena of Nazi Germany, might we not equally be vulnerable to artful and tendentious attacks in the politics of our own experience? Psycho-analysts have almost unanimously thought that we are so vulnerable. Ronald Fairbairn (1952) speaks of an internal saboteur – a subsidiary ego that sets itself against a person's creative and libidinal self. Herbert Rosenfeld (1971) speaks of 'destructive narcissism', describing states of mind in which the whole self becomes temporarily identified with a destructive self that aims to triumph over life and creativity, sometimes taking the form of a powerful internal gang. Donald Meltzer (1973) has described the tyranny that such a part may exercise over a person, presenting itself in the guise of a friend or protector and preventing the development of respect and admiration for others by issuing a stream of slanderous propaganda, while John Steiner (1982) emphasises the way in which a healthy part of the self may knowingly collude in allowing itself to be taken over by the narcissistic gang.

Taking a developmental point of view, analysts have explored two major and overlapping areas of enquiry. Under the general rubric of 'narcissism' come the problems posed by the differentiation of self from other, subject from object, and the relation between different parts in the structure of the self, which form one area of study; while the strategies for dealing with mental pain or anxiety form the other. These are often called 'defence mechanisms', but more plainly stated as 'lies' (either black or white) a person tells himself in order to avoid confrontation with the painful, hard edge of reality.

Clearly we are studying the roots of violence in both cases, for any failure to differentiate self from object simultaneously lays the basis for a failure to respect the integrity of another person. This is illustrated on a horrifying scale by the justifications allegedly submitted by Susan Atkins, a member of the Manson family, after the murder of Sharon Tate. When asked whether it bothered her to have killed a pregnant woman, she reportedly replied (Bugliosi and Gentry 1974): 'Well, I thought you understood. I loved her, and in order for me to kill her I was killing part of myself when I killed her.' As part of a new society elected to go all over the world killing people at random and executing them in order to release them from this earth, Atkins explained: 'You have to have a real love in your heart to do this for people'.

Defence mechanisms are of course the very means employed to cover up this failure to respect boundaries and smooth away the abrasive edge of otherness. When embracing the truth exacts a high price in terms of confrontation with painful affects, we are always in danger of succumbing to propaganda that seeks to transform our perception of reality.

I want to emphasise that these concepts are descriptive. They do not account for the origin of violence, but only describe the way that we subjectively experience its manifestations. It might be unpalatable to suppose that there is something irreducibly given about human violence, a point on which both Freud and Einstein (1933) were in absolute agreement, to say nothing of the Catholic Church! But if it be true that man has within him a lust for hatred and destruction, though again it explains nothing, it does at least suggest that we may have to cope *ab initio* with the consequences of our own destructiveness.

Melanie Klein (1958) observed in her analytical work with young children a constant struggle between an irrepressible urge to destroy their objects and a desire to preserve them, a conflict to which Oscar Wilde gave poetic expression in the *Ballad of Reading Gaol* (1898) when he wrote:

'Yet each man kills the thing he loves,
by each let this be heard,
Some do it with a bitter look,
Some with a flattering word,
The coward does it with a kiss,
The brave man with a sword.'

For the child, such conflict creates a situation of harrowing anxiety. This is how Donald Meltzer (1973) has described it:

'The child's struggle to pursue his relations to his love objects, both internal and external, involves him in problems that bring into focus the attributes of courage, for time and time again the child will fail to preserve good faith at the level of the depressive position and will be faced with the pains of guilt, remorse, unworthiness and shame. Time and again his love will bring in its wake increments of painful worry, loneliness and jealousy, during separation. When we understand how dearly little children must pay for their love relations in the face of limited self control, it helps us to be patient, to support them with resolution, to protect them from undue hardships or temptations.' (p.34)

Could violence then stem from a failure in courage? Could it represent an attempt to obliterate the pangs of guilt and remorse? I do not mean this in the sense that Freud (1916) first adumbrated in his essay 'Criminals from A Sense of Guilt', for he was talking more about a person committing a crime in order to provoke punishment and thus neutralise his unconscious sense of guilt, whereas I am thinking more in terms of an attempt to annihilate the guilt-provoking object.

We may envisage a vicious circle where such an attempt only succeeds in further damaging the object and thus increasing the anxiety it was intended to eliminate. More attacks ensue and there is an amplification of violent activity; the object is progressively degraded and damaged but refuses to lie down, taking on an increasingly persecutory and horrific aspect with each new insult to which it is subjected. Rosenfeld (1962) describes graphic dream material illustrating the way that intolerance to guilt-provoking persecutory superego figures can lead to unconscious murderous impulses. I find this conceptualisation appealing because it rings true; it squares with the compulsively repetitive nature of much violence, including the baby batterer and the multiple murderer. It makes sense of the kind of overkill with which we are familiar in sadistic murders, and provides us with a psychological point of entry which is familiar to us all from our own experience when trying to work with the perpetrators of violent crime.

In summary, I propose that the violation of meaning is germane to physical violence. Meaning is generated in the mind by a creative process of symbol formation that allows the differences between objects to be preserved while at the same time drawing our attention to novel similarities and links between them. Poetry expands the world of meaning; so that when John Donne, pleading in the voice of a flea who has sucked blood from both himself and his lady, says:

> 'Though use make you apt to kill me
> Let not to that self-murder added be
> And sacrilege, three sinnes in killing three,'

our mental life is enriched.

Conversely psychological violence attacks meaning by destroying the links between objects (Bion 1959) or obliterating the differences. The result is a form of concrete thinking where emotions are eliminated, and nothing matters because everything is the same. When asked by a grand jury the meaning of the word 'pig' or 'pigs', after having scrawled them in the victim's blood, a member of the Manson family replied '"Pig" was a word used to describe the establishment. But you must understand that all words had no meaning to us.'

7

Psychoanalysis
The Third Culture?

In his 1959 Rede lecture, C. P. Snow suggested that a division existed in intellectual society between two cultures. He pointed to a surprisingly wide and deep gulf in attitudes, standards, patterns of behaviour, common approaches and assumptions that had grown between scientists and those educated in the arts; with literary intellectuals at one pole and physical scientists at the other. He described how highly intelligent people, standing on either side of this gulf were unable to communicate because they had little understanding of each other's discipline. Each group was isolated in its own world with its own language. Snow felt that this division unnecessarily impoverished our lives; he felt that science and art could be mutually enriching if they were brought together and 'assimilated along with, and as part and parcel of, the whole of our mental experience' (Snow 1959, p.16).

Psychoanalysis is not and never has been easy to define. It comprises both a clinical method and a way of looking at the mind – a technique, perhaps an art and a body of systematic observations, perhaps a science. It exists in the world of ideas and is kept alive as a growing and developing entity by those who study and practise it. Though it remains rooted in the work of Freud, it can now no longer be solely identified with his writing, nor are its practitioners limited to the membership of psychoanalytic institutes (Rycroft 1985). It belongs to humanity for the benefit of mankind, not to any establishment or professional guild; and it follows that what it has to offer should be available to stimulate the imagination and inform the thinking and practice of contemporary social workers. It represents perhaps a 'third culture'.

But what does psychoanalysis have to offer? Clearly it is concerned with human mentality and behaviour, but it is not this concern which distinguishes psychoanalysis from other branches of enquiry. As Gilbert Ryle long ago pointed out in his book *The Concept of Mind*, historians, philologists, literary critics, dramatists, novelists and many others have for thousands of years been studying the deeds, words, opinions, thoughts, feelings, habits, weaknesses and strengths of men and women; which alone deserve the title 'mental phenomena'. In modern times, too, scientific psychologists, underpinning their work with a positivistic empiricist philosophy, have made determined efforts to apply the experimental method to the study of mental events.

Psychoanalysis, however, is none of these things; and if we wish to understand the special contribution that it has to make we must look not to its subject matter, but to its method and its conceptual framework. The web of psychoanalytic knowledge hangs delicately by a thread from its central concept 'transference', while the psychoanalytical method is designed to create optimal conditions for the development of the relationship which this concept denotes. Its epistemology consists in the study of precisely what inferences can be drawn from the experiences occurring in the consulting room.

THE PSYCHOANALYTICAL METHOD

The roots of the psychoanalytical method, as it is practised now, reach back to the turn of the century and can be seen most clearly in Freud's 'Fragment of an Analysis of a Case of Hysteria' familiarly known as 'Dora'. This case is as compelling to study today as it plainly was to Freud in 1901: and it is evident from the following exultant passage that he felt it had led him to a major discovery:

> 'When I set myself the task of bringing to light what human beings keep hidden within them, not by the compelling power of hypnosis, but by observing what they say and what they show, I thought the task was a harder one than it really is. He that has eyes to see and ears to hear may convince himself that no mortal can keep a secret. If his lips are silent, he chatters with his finger-tips; betrayal oozes out of him at every pore. And thus the task of making conscious the most hidden recesses of the mind is one which it is quite possible to accomplish. (*Standard Edition* vol. 7, pp.77–8)

What was it that Freud had discovered? On the face of it as he pointed out the case seemed a medical commonplace, hardly worth presenting: an 18-year-old girl with a long history of nervous cough, shortness of breath, loss of voice and possible migraines in childhood had become withdrawn and depressed. She had consulted many doctors over the years, all of whom had been unable to cure her symptoms; and she had as a consequence developed a lofty contempt for medical efforts. Nevertheless, when she left a suicidal note in a place where her parents would find it, and subsequently after an altercation with her father appeared to have some kind of convulsive fit, they insisted she came to Freud for treatment.

Dora's father was convinced that her symptoms were linked with an episode alleged to have occurred when she was sixteen and spending the summer holiday with old family friends, the Ks, by a lake in the Alps. Dora had told her parents that Herr K made a sexual advance towards her, causing her to cut short the vacation and return home: but when confronted with this, Herr K totally denied it, insisting that the episode was a figment of the girl's imagination. Dora herself recounted to Freud an even earlier episode in which, when she was fourteen, Herr K had invited her to his office, ostensibly to watch a Church fete. He had engineered a situation whereby they would be alone together and taken advantage of it to suddenly steal a passionate kiss on the lips. According to Dora, at this point she felt an intense feeling of disgust, tore herself free and rushed out into the street. Nevertheless they continued to meet on social occasions without any mention of the secret happenings. The situation was further complicated by Dora's conviction that her father suffered from venereal disease and was having an affair with Frau K.

Freud concluded that Dora's own sexuality had been aroused by these events, and that the symptoms represented a symbolic transformation of her desires. At one point in the treatment it became clear that Dora was worried she had inherited her father's venereal disease, which was the cause of her persistent longstanding white vaginal discharge. When Freud suggested that this leucorrhoea was more likely to be due to masturbation, she denied any knowledge of such a practice. Notwithstanding this a few days later she came to an analytical session wearing for the first time a small reticule round her waist. As she lay on Freud's sofa talking, he noticed that she kept playing with it, opening it, putting her finger into it, shutting it again, and so on. He was left in no doubt as to the meaning of this 'symptomatic act' which clearly could be taken to represent masturbation thus confirming his earlier suspicions.

What a person said and did during the consultations began to take on a new light for Freud; he saw that a patient's communications should be taken not only at their face value, but also as symbolic representations carrying hidden messages. More than this, he began to see that people not only gave expression to their desires in this way, but that they were driven inexorably to do so. As the philosopher Susan Langer (1942) put it:

'The great contribution of Freud to the philosophy of mind has been the realisation that human behaviour is not only a food-getting strategy, but is also a language; that every move is a gesture. Symbolization is both an end and an instrument … The fact is I believe that it did not originate purely in the service of other activities. It is a primary interest, and may require a sacrifice of other ends, just as the imperative demand for food or sex-life may necessitate sacrifices under different conditions.' (p.51)

It was but a short step from this realisation for the idea to suggest itself to Freud that he himself had been used by Dora for purposes of symbolic representation. Thus, it dawned on him that not only had he replaced her father in her imagination at the beginning of the analysis but that her sudden termination of the treatment represented a re-enactment of her flight from Herr K's house; an action Freud had previously interpreted as a wish to escape from the expression of her own feelings of sexual attraction towards Herr K. It was borne in on Freud that the psychoanalytical setting presented an ideal theatre for the symbolic re-enactment of hidden conflicts of this sort.

Here then was a methodological tool of immense importance for it now seemed that the old 'archaeological' model of analysis, rooting around in the patient's recollections for 'traumatic events', could be superseded by a new and far more powerful source of information. As Freud put it in his seminal essay on 'Remembering, Repeating and Working-Through' (1914):

> 'we may say that the patient does not *remember* anything of what he has forgotten and repressed, but acts it out. He reproduces it not as a memory but as an action; he *repeats* it, without, of course, knowing that he is repeating it. For instance, the patient does not say that he remembers that he used to be defiant and critical towards his parent's authority; instead, he behaves in that way to the doctor. He does not remember how he came to a helpless and hopeless deadlock in his infantile sexual researches; but he produces a mass of confused dreams and associations; complains that he cannot succeed in anything and asserts that he is fated never to carry through what he undertakes. He does not remember having been intensely ashamed of certain sexual activities and afraid of them being found out; but he makes it clear that he is ashamed of the treatment on which he is now embarked and tries to keep it secret from everybody.' [italics original] (p.150)

With this kind of data to be plumbed, the aims of the psychoanalytical method became clearer: namely, to provide a kind of playground in which the compulsion to repeat earlier experiences could be given expression and then thought about. Thomas Szasz (1963) put it succinctly when he said: 'Just as the pre-Freudian physician was ineffective partly because he remained a fully "real" person, so the psychoanalyst may be ineffective if he remains a fully "symbolic" object. The analytic situation requires the therapist to function as both. Without these conditions "analysis" cannot take place.'

A setting that allowed the creation of an intermediate world somewhere between pure phantasy and real life was required, and the techniques for achieving this had to be developed. These quite simply depended on the analyst's stability, reliability, tolerance, restraint, and friendly non-judgemental attitude combined with an uncompromising determination to search for the truth.

No special skill in reasoning is needed to see immediately a formidable logical objection to this psychoanalytical method. What if Freud were wrong? How can we be sure that when Dora played with her reticule, Freud was correct in imputing the meaning of masturbation or that when she suddenly broke off her treatment with him she was re-enacting her flight from Herr K's house? Freud (1905) himself raises the question when he says: 'Transference is the one thing the presence of which has to be detected almost without assistance and with only the slightest clues to go upon, while at the same time the risk of making arbitrary inferences has to be avoided' (p.116).

To put it another way, what principles can establish whether a particular interpretation of the meaning of a given symbol is correct? An interesting paradigm for this problem is created when a dictionary definition of a word is challenged in the courts. If for example a dictionary asserts that the meaning of the word 'Hoover' is a 'vacuum cleaner' and the Hoover manufacturing company contest this interpretation on the grounds that the word refers only to those cleaning machines manufactured by themselves, the publishers of the dictionary will be required to prove that their definition is correct. In order to do so they must turn to 'usage', for there is no final arbiter, no other source that can authoritatively adjudicate the meaning of a symbol. Nor can this meaning be fixed, since usage changes with the elapse of time. They will have to search for citations in current newspapers and books that demonstrate beyond doubt from their context that the word can be and is being used in a particular way.

Freud follows a similar procedure, adducing evidence from usage: fairy-tales, literature, jokes, slang, other languages, roots of words, slips of the tongue, and contextual settings. All are brought into play in order to add weight to his interpretations. It is certainly not difficult on this basis to demonstrate that a reticule can mean the female genital. Indeed, Freud produces an amusing and convincing account of another of his patients bringing out a small ivory box during a consultation ostensibly to refresh herself with a sweet. Finding the box difficult to open, in a state of agitation, she eventually handed it to Freud; 'It must mean something very special' he said, since it was the first time he had seen it although she had been coming for more than a year. She immediately replied, 'I always have this box about me; I take it with me wherever I go.' Freud (1905) comments: 'She did not calm down until I pointed out to her with a laugh how well her words were adapted to quite another meaning. The box, like the reticule and the Jewel Case, was once again only a substitute for the shell of Venus, for the female genitals' (p.77).

But a symbol can be used in an idiosyncratic way; how can we be sure that in any particular case we have arrived at a correct understanding of its meaning? The answer, I think, is that we cannot be sure, nor can we ever prove or disprove a meaning; for meanings are no more susceptible to the methods of Newtonian physics than billiard balls are to an understanding of dinner-table conversation! To quote Langer (1942) once again:

'If we follow the methods of natural science our psychology tends to run into physiology, histology and genetics; we move further and further away from those problems which we ought to be approaching. That signifies that the generative idea which gave rise to physics and chemistry and all their progeny, technology, medicine, biology does not contain any vivifying concepts for the humanistic sciences. The physicists' scheme so faithfully emulated by generations of psychologists, epistemologists and aestheticians is probably blocking their progress, defeating possible insights by its prejudicial force. The scheme is not false, it is perfectly reasonable, but it is bootless for the study of mental phenomena. It does not engender leading questions and excite a constructive imagination, as it does in physical researches. Instead of a method, it inspires a militant methodology.' (p.24)

However, although it may be beside the point to attempt to prove or disprove the correctness of a given interpretation, it does not follow that all interpretations are of equal value. We may continue to ask whether our interpretation adequately covers the data at hand, whether it enriches or impoverishes the symbolic universe, whether it fits into a consistent pattern and articulates with other meanings; and though we can never prove it, still it may or may not be true and has to be taken account of in our deliberations.

PSYCHOANALYTICAL CONCEPTS

Most of us are exquisitely sensitive to any failure in the environment to recognise our qualities or to take account of our needs. This is not surprising as we all start life with a multitude of needs, a minimal ability to communicate them and a total dependence on others for their satisfaction. It seems obvious therefore that early frustration must be an inevitable part of the human condition. Just how this is experienced by any particular baby would remain forever unknowable and a matter for speculation unless it were true that the examination of transference in the psychoanalytical situation really tells us something about the past.

It is idle to ruminate on this problem however, since there is no way it can be resolved. What seems more useful is to recognise that transference is a descriptive term, allowing us to outline the regressive phenomena that obtrude so forcefully on attention during the heat of the psychoanalytical moment. Transference is a special experience, an event in the here and now. We say that transference love is infantile, and mean that it seems to us to have the qualities we would not be surprised to find in an infant's emotional life, if only we had direct access to it.

If *transference* is the name given to the process whereby the analyst comes to be used as a living symbol for the reanimation of unconscious infantile conflicts, a careful study of this process should be able to tell us something about the way in which symbols are formed. Fortunately, the analyst is able to make use of his own subjective responses in order to carry out this investigation. This activity is essentially introspective and is set in motion and nurtured during the course of his experience as a patient. It is this self-analytic capacity that enables him to examine his *counter-transference* and use it as a tool for discovery (Heinmann 1960; Racker 1968).

The dramaturgical analogy I alluded to earlier helps us to a better under-standing of this. It is as if there exists in the mind of the patient a play of which he himself is unaware yet which he inadvertently directs. The cast consists of a wide range of people and objects in his life, but gradually, as he becomes involved in the analytical process, a new performance is produced within the confines of the consulting room. The psychoanalyst is required to take many roles in this play, and by listening to the instructions of the unconscious director and above all recognising his own emotional responses, he slowly comes to unravel both the script of the play and the character of the director. He is then in a position to report back to his patient what he has noticed and discuss the intricacies of the plot. Needless to say he must refrain from actually taking part in the drama!

This, then, is what a modern psychoanalyst is able to reconstruct: not so much a veridical version of the past but a fiction that makes the present intelligible and adds coherence to a person's picture of himself. He is a kind of poet rather than a kind of archaeologist (Spence 1982; Kermode 1985).

While with adult patients the arcane drama of transference often requires laborious effort to demonstrate, since it offends against 'common sense' (Money-Kyrle 1956), in material derived from child psychoanalysis we can see the process displayed with graphic clarity. Consider the following short example from the analysis of a very troubled six-year-old girl treated by Melanie Klein (1932).

'Erna began her play by taking a small carriage which stood on the little table among the other toys and letting it run towards me. She declared that she had come to fetch me. But she put a toy woman in the carriage instead and added a toy man. The two loved and kissed one another and drove up and down all the time. Next a toy man in another carriage collided with them, ran over them and killed them, and then roasted and ate them up. Another time the fight had a different ending and the attacking toy man was thrown down; but the woman helped him and comforted him. She got a divorce from her first husband and married the new one. This third person was given the most various parts to play in Erna's games. For instance, the original man and his wife were in a house which they were defending against a burglar; the third person was the burglar and slipped in. The house burnt down, the man and woman burnt and the third person was the only one left. Then again the third person was a brother who came on a visit; but while embracing the woman he bit her nose off.' (p.36)

From this and other material, Mrs Klein was able to infer that the little man, the third person, was none other than Erna herself, while of course the woman in the carriage, said by Erna to be Mrs Klein, clearly also represented Erna's mother. Erna had expressed her destructive wishes towards the parents' intercourse, as well as her primitive wish to eat them. At the same time she had also shown the intricate and paradoxical organisation of her conflict; for while she clearly wished to oust her father and marry her mother (*negative Oedipus complex*), who was portrayed as helpful and comforting in one scenario, she attacked her unmercifully in another. Later still, she demonstrated her wish to be rid of mother altogether and to win father (*direct Oedipus complex*). Thus she made a toy teacher throw down his book and dance with his girl pupil, kissing and embracing her. Then she suddenly asked Mrs Klein if she would allow a marriage between teacher and pupil.

During the course of the analysis (Klein 1929) Erna often required Mrs Klein to play the part of a child, while she took the role of mother and teacher. At those times the child had to undergo fantastic tortures and humiliations. She was constantly spied on, and her parents ganged up against her, while she herself spied upon and tormented others. At other times Erna herself played the part of the child, and the game generally ended in her escaping persecution, becoming rich and powerful, being made a queen and taking cruel revenge. But this consistently led to a reaction, in the form of deep depression, anxiety, and bodily exhaustion.

With the advent of Melanie Klein's play technique of child analysis, we can see that a vast world of unconscious child phantasy was laid patent, a noumenal world in which all of us live, every bit as real as the phenomenal world of external reality. Careful observation then enabled Mrs Klein to make use of this rich source in formulating some new and far-reaching ideas. The process of symbol construction, in its most primitive form, began to be comprehended in terms of the infant's need to cope with overwhelming anxiety (Klein 1930). Where the world was unacceptably threatening, it seemed that from childhood onwards we altered it by the simple expedient of omnipotent phantasy.

Of course analysts had long been familiar with the concept of infantile omnipotence and hallucinatory wish-fulfilment – Freud's *pleasure principle* (1911) – for the way we make reality tolerable, the distortions we impose upon reality are leitmotifs in psychoanalytical thinking. But this had previously always been conceptualised as a unitary process concerning the magical experience of dealing with frustration through hallucination of a good and gratifying object.

What impressed Klein again and again was the spontaneous creation, as in Erna's case of two groups of symbols, representing both extremely good *and* extremely bad characteristics: the complicated mixtures of qualities inherent in real people appeared to be reorganised into much simpler schematic structures. Children, it seemed, created their own gods and devils without the help of organised religion! It is easy to see why there should be a need for powerful gods that can comfort us and temper anxiety arising from helplessness, but it is more difficult to understand the necessity for devils. What Mrs Klein saw was the unavoidable duality of the phenomenon, that for every idealised object generated a reciprocal diabolic object was of necessity brought into being, the existence of which had perforce to be denied. 'Splitting' was intimately linked with *idealisation* and *introjection* of the good and its correlative, *denial* and *projection* of the bad. More than this, our adult characters were seen to be rooted in these fundamental processes, and to depend for development on their successful accomplishment (Klein 1946).

The formation of mind was thus placed in a familiar age old pattern of creative myth. Just as the book of Genesis describes the creation of a firmament as the first step in giving form to chaos and void, so Klein in her psychoanalytical poem saw differentiation in the *paranoid-schizoid position* as the foundation of psychological growth. Failure to make a clear distinction between love and hate, led to further difficulties in distinguishing between self and object, inside and outside – a state of confusion; while an excessively profound split inhibited later integration and carried the danger of a complete divorce form external reality. Adequate splitting however modulated anxiety and allowed progress to occur towards a greater tolerance of imperfect things. The *idealised object* could then give way to a mere *good object* or in other words an object whose mixed qualities were recognised and acknowledged but whose 'badness' had been forgiven. This process was accompanied by a profound change in values. Meltzer (1973) saw it in the following way:

> 'Where this primary splitting and idealisation of infant self and objects has satisfactorily taken place, where the parental services are reasonably adequate, where neither jealousy, envy nor intolerance to mental pain are excessive, a miraculous and beautiful thing tends to take place, known in flat scientific jargon as "the phenomenology of the depressive position". In the language of life, tender concern for the welfare of the beloved object tends to supersede selfish concern for the comfort and safety of the self. The capacity for sacrifice emerges – babies wait for their feeds instead of screaming, leave off sucking when more is still available in breast or bottle, try to control their sphincters to spare the mother, bear separation despite worry. Out of obedience, goodness emerges; out of competitiveness, the capacity to work; out of toleration of deprivation, pride in development.' (p.33)

The description of these developmental processes had important consequences for the programme of psychoanalysis. Clearly what analysts were able to 'see' being re-enacted in the transference depended to a large extent on how they viewed the original infantile course of events. Where Freud had focused on the vicissitudes of biologically determined instinctual phases and the negotiation of the Oedipus triangle leading to 'genital' character formation, a process driven by *castration anxiety*, Klein shifted the emphasis on to the subtle interplay of projective and introjective processes in earliest infancy, leading to the *depressive position* – a state of mind characterised by the capacity to bear remorseful feelings and the willing acceptance of the wish to make reparation.

THE AIMS OF PSYCHOANALYSIS

The therapeutic aims of psychoanalysis have been reformulated over the years in the light of clinical experience, and in order to keep pace with changes in the model of the mind being used. In the early days, Freud was able to state its aim quite simply – to make what was unconscious conscious. This was in keeping with the relatively simple topographical model he had put forward (Freud 1915c) dividing the mind into two regions – unconscious and conscious – between which was located a censor whose job it was to prevent unacceptable wishes moving from one place to the other. It also squared with the early clinical experiences described in *Studies on Hysteria*. Anna O. Breuer's hysterical young patient, suffered among other things from horrifying hallucinations of death's heads and skeletons during the day, but she was able to cure herself by inducing a state of auto-hypnotism at night which she called 'clouds', in which she narrated in detail her daytime troubles so that she woke up calm and cheerful. It seemed consistent to hypothesise that the hypnotic state had allowed consciousness access to some of the contents of the unconscious and in doing so had somehow disarmed them.

This model of the mind, however, was inadequate to cover the burgeoning clinical data Freud was accumulating. In particular resistance to free association, masochism, and melancholia presented problems for the topographical model. According to the model, the 'unconscious' was conflict-free, unaware of contradictions, and interested only in seeking pleasure; censorious and repressing forces, however were supposed to be located only in the sphere of the 'conscious'. But Freud was regularly encountering blocks to his clinical investigations of which his patients were quite unaware, and punishment seeking behaviour which forced him to postulate an 'unconscious sense of guilt'.

Eventually he lost interest in the distinction conscious/unconscious (somewhat surprisingly warning us to emancipate ourselves from the importance of the 'symptom' of consciousness), and reformulated his model in terms of the relationship between three mental agencies or structures known to the English speaking world as the ego, the id, and the superego (1923). It is true that he continued to speak of the id being unconscious and the superego dipping down into the unconscious, but the primary concern was now clearly the nature of the relationship between them. In this model, the ego was portrayed as a servant required to work for three masters and constantly torn between the demands of the id for instinctual gratification, the demands of the superego for obedience and renunciation, and the limitations imposed by external reality.

Symptoms were now seen as arising from an imbalance between the three mental structures – for example, an excessively punitive superego, or an excessively weak ego; and Freud, in a famous passage, was able to liken the work of psychoanalysis in strengthening the ego to that of land reclamation:

'Its intention is, indeed, to strengthen the ego, to make it more independent of the superego, to widen its field of perception and enlarge its organisation, so that it can appropriate fresh portions of the id. Where id was, there ego shall be. It is a work of culture – not unlike the draining of the Zuider Zee.' (1933)

But how was this to be accomplished? How, for instance to render the ego more independent of the superego, well known to be extremely severe in small children even when their parents are mild and benign?

Using Klein's conceptualisation of the superego as an archaic internal object, essentially influenced by the child's own aggression, amplified in a vicious circle of projection and re-introjection, Strachey (1934) was able to come up with an answer. The analyst's role was to act as an auxiliary superego that could help to break the vicious circle by making 'mutative interpretations':

'If all goes well the patient's ego will become aware of the contrast between the aggressive character of his feelings and the real nature of the analyst, who does not behave like the patients 'good' and 'bad' archaic objects. The patient, that is to say, will become aware of a distinction between his archaic object and the real external object. The interpretation has now become a mutative one since it has produced a breach in the neurotic vicious circle. For the patient, having become aware of the lack of aggressiveness in the real external object, will be able to diminish his own aggressiveness; the new object he introjects will be less aggressive, and consequently the aggressiveness of his superego will be diminished.' (p.283)

Note that in this formulation the analyst's role is essentially a negative one, he facilitates change by *not* behaving in accord with expectations derived from the patient's unconscious phantasies. The disjunction thus created stimulates mental work on the part of the patient to accommodate the 'reality' he is confronted with. He has to 'adjust' his phantasies. But this model also only goes part of the way towards a satisfactory description of the psychoanalytical relationship. It was left to Wilfred Bion (1973, 1977) to provide a fuller account.

Perhaps as a result of his work with psychotic patients (who were not prepared to adjust their phantasies so easily), Bion was led to a more positive conception both of the role of the mother in the development of infant mentation and of course of the analyst in the transference relationship. In this view, when mental pain arises it can either be dealt with by being converted into thoughts and symbols (what Bion called alpha function), which can then be subject to further modification by the process of 'thinking'; or it can be evacuated in its raw non-symbolic form (beta elements), and transferred into another object. What this means in terms of infant care is that where the child lacks the ability to transform pain into thoughts, the mother can do this work for him and thus actively help the development of mind. In order to accomplish this, of course, she has to tolerate a great deal of pain herself. She has to 'contain' and 'metabolise' the infant's projections.

This is how Bion (1973) imagines the situation of a baby who is very upset and perhaps afraid of some impending disaster, which it expresses by crying:

> 'Suppose the mother picks up the baby and comforts it, is not at all disorganised or distressed, but makes some soothing response. The distressed infant can feel that by its screams or yells, it has expelled those feelings of impending disaster into the mother. The mother's response can be felt to detoxicate the evacuation of the infant; the sense of impending disaster is modified by the mother's reaction and can then be taken back into itself by the baby. Having got rid of a sense of impending disaster, the infant gets back something which is far more tolerable. Susan Isaacs has described a situation in which the baby could be heard saying something like 'oo el, oo el', which the mother recognised as an imitation of herself saying 'well, well'. In that way the infant was able to feel comforted by a good mother inside and could make reassuring, comforting noises to itself exactly as if the mother was there all the time.'

But the mother is only able to do this by virtue of her own capacity for 'alpha function'. If this is impaired she will react irritably and anxiously towards her child; forcing the infant to take back into itself the sense of impending disaster, which only worsens the original situation and sets up a vicious circle. Once again we can extrapolate to the analytical situation, seeing the function of the analyst as analogous to that of the mother. He must break the vicious circle but this time actively, using his own capacity for giving symbolic expression to inchoate pain and thus bringing it within the domain of thought.

When Melanie Klein transformed Freud's structural agencies into 'internal objects' located in an interior world of phantasy she had clearly taken a step that profoundly altered the nature of psycho-analysis both as theory and therapy (Meltzer 1984; Wisdom 1984). She had thrust psychoanalysis from its closed system of scientific energetics into the open system of an imaginative, artistic discipline, and in doing so laid the foundation for contemporary object-relational psychology. It remained for Wilfred Bion and others to develop this open system of imagination and hone it into a clinical tool capable of helping people give form to their most ineffable anxieties and thus to suffer them.

8

Anxiety and Depression in the Workplace
Cause or Effect?

There appear to be two schools of thought regarding the effect of work on mental well-being. Briefly stated one holds that work is good for you while the other states that it is not. This conflict much preoccupied the Victorians and the issues emerge clearly from an examination of mid nineteenth century writings.

As an example of the first I can do no better than quote Thomas Carlyle:

'– a man perfects himself by working. Foul jungles are cleared away, fair seed fields rise instead, and stately cities; and withal the man himself first ceases to be a jungle and foul unwholesome desert thereby. Consider how, even in the meanest sorts of labour, the whole soul of a man is composed into a kind of real harmony, the instant he sets himself to work! Doubt, Desire, Sorrow, Remorse, Indignation, Despair itself, all these like hell-fire dogs lie beleaguering the soul of the poor dayworker, as of every man: but he bends himself with free valour against his task, and all these are stilled, all these shrink murmuring far off into their caves.

The man is now a man. The blessed glow of Labour in him, is it not as purifying fire, wherein all poison is burnt up, and of sour smoke itself there is made bright blessed flame!' (1843, III, 12, 200)

It seems doubtful therefore that Carlyle would have prescribed time off work for a person suffering from melancholia. Clearly in his view work was the cure and not the cause of mental ills. It was the means by which man most profoundly fulfilled himself.

What then of the contrary notion? – the harmful effects of work on a person's mental state. They are probably most eloquently stated by Karl Marx writing at the same time (1844), in his concept of 'alienation'.

'The more the worker expends himself in work the more powerful becomes the world of objects which he creates in face of himself, and the poorer he himself becomes in his inner life, the less he belongs to himself.' (p.83) and again:

> 'In what does this alienation of labour consist? First, that the work is *external* to the worker, that it is not a part of his nature, that consequently he does not fulfil himself in his work but denies himself, has a feeling of misery, not of well-being, does not develop freely a physical and mental energy, but is physically exhausted and mentally debased. The worker therefore finds himself at home only during his leisure, whereas at work he feels homeless. His work is not voluntary but imposed, *forced labour*. It is not the satisfaction of a need but only a *means* of satisfying other needs. Its alien character is clearly shown by the fact that as soon as there is no physical or other compulsion it is avoided like the plague.' [italics original] (p.86)

Of course I have set up here an artificial dichotomy, for it is clear you will agree (together with Marx) that under certain conditions work may be fulfilling and therapeutic while where the circumstances and social relations are not propitious alienation will result. On this view anxiety and depression in the workplace will be seen as a function of the social relations of the worker *vis-à-vis* his employer, and the cure for problems may rest in an alteration of these relations. Revolutionary activity may be called for if the relationship of the worker to the means of production are to be changed, or if the necessary social changes are considered less radical piecemeal reorganisation on a lesser scale may be advocated. Every change both within an organisation and in society at large which alters the locus of power and decision-making, specifies managerial responsibilities, creates systems for monitoring the worker's activity and output, and by determining and shaping his work inevitably affects his mental state or in old-fashioned terms his 'morale'. So much is obvious and it follows that there is little point in making vague generalisations in this area. How and in what direction a person's mental well-being is affected by social circumstances is an enormous question and only becomes meaningful if smaller specific questions regarding particular people in particular places are asked.

I want here to take a more psychological perspective and to outline some of the ways in which an individual may make use of his social environment in the workplace to give expression to his own inner history and conflicts, which may then appear to present themselves as mental illnesses. The workplace may be regarded as a large theatre in which an individual is provided amongst his colleagues and other contacts with a multiplicity of actors; in large organisations a 'cast of thousands' whom he can enrol in 're-producing' his own personal drama. It is commonplace knowledge nowadays, highlighted by Freud's concept of the 'repetition compulsion', that we tend to repeat in our human relations the same problematic situations over and over again. The wife who repeatedly selects husbands who batter her, or the man who seems to have to self-destruct and prevent himself from being successful whenever the chance arises are gross examples of this process. So it is not surprising that the workplace provides an ideal setting for inner conflicts such as these to manifest themselves.

The following brief vignette of a case in which I was recently involved provides an illustration:

'A middle aged probation officer presented to her GP complaining of being run down and tearful. She had lost weight and suffered sleep disturbance and a lack of libido. By the time I saw her she had already been off work for two weeks and been prescribed Amitriptyline 10 mg at night increasing slowly to 50 mgs nocte, which she had not taken.

She was an intelligent and attractive mother of three children and it appeared that her depression and anxiety state was related to a particular situation at work. According to her GP she had complained about the quality of a particular male colleague's work and had felt inadequately supported in her complaint by the woman who was her immediate superior, and by her employers as a whole. She was particularly bitter about her relationship with the man at work whom she felt scived off leaving her to do all the work and carry all the responsibility.

It was also clear to her doctor that her relationship with her husband reflected this situation. She said 'he comes into the house expecting the family to run round him, and makes remarks like "Why should I wash up when there are three children around?"'

What we did not know at this stage were the details of her early history and the pattern of her character as it had unfolded over the years. As I got to know her it appeared that she had been adopted in infancy and brought up by her adoptive parents as their natural child. Her mother who was a police officer was a dominant woman who dealt with all the bills in the house while her father was a quiet man who suffered from severe migraine. However, mother was frightened of hospitals and so, she added, it had always fallen to her as a child to take her father to hospital in order to give him moral support. Similarly, when she had broken her arm in her teens, her mother had been unable to support her, but instead told father to accompany her to hospital which she indignantly refused, saying she would go on her own. Her sister too came in for criticism. She was apparently brighter than my patient and had been encouraged by her parents to pursue her education, eventually qualifying as a doctor, but according to my patient had not pulled her weight when mother was ill a few years previously and needed nursing. Instead my patient, who had never been favoured by mother, was left to look after her in her hour of need. It appeared that over the years she had developed a kind of militant

independence and competence which rested on a basis of inner rage that
nobody could do anything for her therefore she had better do it for herself.

She could never forgive her husband for his behaviour during her last
confinement. He had gone off to another town to do some work just before
the baby was due. When the baby was born she told the hospital not to
get in touch with him.

When I asked this lady what her job consisted of she replied that she
was just 'a general dogsbody'. I think I have said enough to give you the
flavour of the case.

It seemed clear that her problems with the man at work fell into a pattern
of life-long resentment at being hard-done by and 'taken for granted' –
that both her husband and her colleague also represented her adoptive
parents whom she felt had failed her, and of course her biological parents
who had in fact abandoned her.'

It was no wonder that this lady with her counter-dependent personality had
pushed aside her antidepressant medication, nor that she was so extraordinarily
bitter when the management at work refused to uphold her complaints against
the male colleague. This must have seemed to her like a major betrayal of the
emotional truth, for the work situation was plainly being used as a hanger on
which her internal conflict could be suspended and brought to life.

Some brief psychotherapy sessions in which these problems were aired
coupled with encouragement to return to work seemed to be helpful. Eventually
after nine weeks' sick leave she resumed her job and was a good deal more
cheerful. She was still unsure however how much to expect from her husband
and how much of her problem was due to the 'chip' which she so clearly now
recognised was on her shoulder.

Does this mean that the work situation can be exonerated as a causal factor
in her depression and that her male colleague was innocent of any misbehaviour?
By no means. I discovered later from impeccable sources that he was a well known
'moonlighter' – famous at work for skiving and shirking his duties. Clearly
management too had been turning a blind eye to this for a long time and had let
my patient down by refusing to back up her complaints and confront the
individual concerned.

As with many similar problems where a person's early experiences are
re-enacted in a work situation the characters chosen are often type-cast so that
the 'cap often fits'.

What is the message that can be gleaned from all this?

There is no simple answer. Working conditions are part and parcel of a
person's total life situation. They provide a complex external social setting which

may support or undermine a person's inner sense of mental well-being. Above all, people inevitably make use of their work environment and relationships to re-enact and work through patterns of feelings and emotions which are deeply unconscious. In doing so they imbue their colleagues and workmates with qualities which may be warranted but also carry a deeply irrational component. Sensitivity to these issues is helpful in understanding and managing situations which present as anxiety, tension and depression in the workplace.

9

Close Encounters in General Practice
Experiences of a Psychotherapy Liaison Team

In recent years, there has been increased interest in establishing closer working relationships between the psychiatric services and general practice (GP). this development has been encouraged by official reports produced by the WHO (1973) and DHSS (1977); in 1982, Williams found, in a nationwide survey of consultant psychiatrists (so far unpublished), that at least 150 were conducting work in a GP setting.

Clinical psychologists (Johnson 1978), social workers, (Graham and Scher 1976), medical and lay psychotherapists (Brook 1978; Temperley 1978), psychiatric nurses, and counsellors (Leopoldt 1979) have also experimented with work in conjunction with primary care teams. Reports of such experiments appearing in the literature naturally tend to stress the advantages of the new arrangements over more traditional ways of working.

Some of these claims are well known: the opportunity to increase communication between GP and psychiatrist; the reduction in stigma for the patient; the convenience of local access to expert help; increased recognition of psychiatric morbidity, as well as improved job satisfaction and rewards for both partners. Mitchell (1983) referring to the natural affinity of psychiatrist and GP stated that:

'They have similar attitudes and philosophies: the cure of the whole person rather than a specific bodily system; the care of the individual in the context of his family, and a concern for the subtle interaction of constitutional, psychological, emotional, and social factors in the genesis of disorder.' (p.100)

But harmonious relationships are difficult to achieve, and by the end of the same article Mitchell warns us that for the liaison to succeed, the specialist must be prepared to:

'... take the risk of exposing himself personally to colleagues who can have a *different* perspective and professional philosophy from his own.' [my italics] (p.106)

Brook (1978), writing about the working relationship between GP and psycho-therapeutic consultant, emphasised the problems:

> 'It cannot be stressed sufficiently that difficulties occur here if the professionals ignore the interpersonal aspects of their working relationships or fail to give them proper consideration.' (pp.37–39)

At Littlemore Hospital, Oxford there has been a long tradition of multi-disciplinary collaboration in community psychiatry; the Ashhurst Clinic, specialising in the psychotherapeutic approach to problems, has been developing close links with GPs over the last ten years (Agerholm 1980). This article describes some of the experiences we have had in carrying out this work. My object is to illustrate something of the difficulties encountered, and to outline for others some of the complex problems arising from both personal and social structures which are likely to occur. I will deal first with events from the early phases, and then with those from the middle period, finally touching on some material related to the ending of an attachment.

THE EARLY PHASES

Wilfred Bion (1961) once remarked apropos of 'therapy groups', that the only cure of which he could speak with certainty was related to a comparatively minor symptom of his own – a belief that groups might take kindly to his efforts. One of the first things we noticed when we began to get involved with GPs was a similar kind of improvement in our mental health! It wasn't simply that we encountered a lack of interest in, or hostility towards, psychiatry – nor was it any kind of overt lack of welcome. Our GPs actively desired and were grateful for the service we were offering; they usually met us in lunch meetings and provided friendly hospitality. What often happened was that the visiting psychotherapist began to feel that his professional practice was being subtly undermined. Circumspection about the referral of patients would give way to profuse apologies and promises for future referrals. Therapists, whose patients rarely missed appointments in other settings, suddenly found that their patients did not turn up, or failed to return for a second interview.

The complexities of the referral process and the importance of ensuring that all parties concerned – patient, GP and therapist – understood and agreed to the action proposed soon became obvious. The GPs had difficulty deciding whom and when to refer. They did not wish to waste our time by referring patients with what appeared to be minor psychological symptoms, and at the same time recognised an eagerness in themselves to dispose quickly of patients with intractable problems. Often, patients who were referred turned out to be en-meshed in an already well established and complex emotional relationship with their doctor, and there was perhaps an inappropriate expectation that by bringing psychotherapeutic expertise to the patient, their co-operation would be automatically achieved.

However, the stigma associated with referral to a psychiatrist in our society and the concomitant implications of moral weakness could not be avoided simply by moving out of the institutional setting. Doctors sometimes went to extraordinary lengths in inventing circumlocutions to describe us, and these difficulties were not confined to any particular practice or to any particular member of the team.

It is commonplace to find that considerable anxiety is generated in a group of people who become aware that a psychiatrist is in their midst. It often takes the form of joking about 'being analysed' or 'having their minds read'. People's behaviour in such a group alters in order to try and prevent themselves from being exposed to the psychiatrist, and sometimes reaches the extreme of actually shunning the psychiatrist completely. The same kind of reaction can be expected from a group of GPs who are exposed to a psychiatrist in their practice for the first time. A fragment of one of my first meetings at a health centre illustrates the kind of initial response I am thinking of:

> 'There seemed to be a good deal of anxiety in the air. After a period of light-hearted banter, I raised a question concerning the way of working we might adopt. There followed much talk by the GPs about giving up prescribing anti-depressants in favour of the patient seeing a psychotherapist from our team. There appeared to be an element of rivalry among the doctors as to who prescribed the least psychotropic medication. The psychotherapist who was attached to the practice was with me at the meeting. He had felt that the GPs were reluctant to refer him patients, but on arrival that day, had been greeted by one of the female partners, who asked him if she could refer somebody. It turned out that the patient was a woman of 60 who feared that she would attack somebody physically, although she showed no outward signs of aggression. My colleague accepted the referral, but during the middle of his first interview with this patient, the door opened and the GP who had made the referral accidentally came in, and withdrew apologising.'

Here, the anxiety in the group of doctors was apparent, and resulted in a certain amount of rivalry between partners as to whom was working in the most psychotherapeutic way. At the same time, the psychotherapist had felt shunned by the lack of referrals that were forthcoming. Psychotherapists work in what might be seen as a privileged way – able to spend long uninterrupted hours with their patients. The referral of a woman with violent tendencies may have been an unconscious acting out of the GP's own feelings towards the therapist. It is, of course, not unusual in the context of general practice for partners to enter each others' rooms during consultations, but equally there may have been an unconscious desire on the part of the GP to find out exactly what went on during the long psychotherapeutic sessions.

In another example from a different practice, a therapist reported that he had been interrupted twice during the course of a session. On one occasion, the GP placed some files on the desk which the therapist was using, and the second time, said that he had forgotten that the therapist was still there. Finally, the therapist found that both he and the patient had been locked into the surgery by the GP, who had gone home. The luckless therapist then had to telephone in order to get both himself and the patient released from the building!

In a third example, a female therapist was attached to an all-male practice. She was welcomed to the practice at a friendly meeting, and one of the senior partners brought a bottle of wine along in her honour. Soon the atmosphere became relaxed and the GPs made some jokes, which expressed their anxiety about 'being analysed' and having their minds read. Then, the doctors began to explain to the therapist the difference between a health centre owned by the health authority and a practice owned by the GPs themselves. 'Owning it ourselves means that we have a licence to do anything we wish' one of them said. Then, pointing to the corridor where the therapist had been offered the use of a consulting room, he added: '... for example, we could set up a massage parlour in the corridor or employ a whore in one of the rooms'!

These examples serve to illustrate how a knowledge of the different ways of working must be achieved at the outset of the relationship, if it is not to be soured by misunderstandings. It is not surprising that the problem of managing unacceptable sexual and violent impulses is never far from the surface in the clinical setting of a doctor's surgery. Often, it influences both the decision made by a practitioner to refer a patient and the subsequent course of therapy, but this may not be acknowledged at the time. In the following example, the patient's problem seems to mirror that of the referring doctor, while the difficulties experienced by the therapist become understandable in the light of later events:

'A female GP referred a man in his early forties because he was having difficulty in his work and had become depressed. Mr G, a university lecturer, had become emotionally entangled with a young female undergraduate. He was seen regularly for about four months, during which time he rejected all the interpretations made by the therapist, out of hand. The therapist found it difficult to feel engaged in the work, but Mr G. said that he felt better, and the therapist was relieved when they agreed a finishing date.

Two years later, Mr G. was once again referred to the therapist. Apparently, his depression had returned, but this time in referring him, the GP passed on a message from the patient to the effect that he was "willing to see the therapist again, but hoped the therapist would change his style and take a more active role". The GP appeared to concur with this, and the therapist began once again to see the patient. The relationship, however, soon deteriorated into the previous pattern, which had seemed so therapeutically barren. The therapist was hard put to understand why the GP had insisted that he see the patient again, when both she and Mr. G felt that he was not providing the desired 'style' of therapy.

In this practice, regular meetings were held with the therapist to discuss cases, and it happened that some months later the subject of 'erotic transference' arose. A male partner in the practice was obviously having a difficulty that he wanted to share. There was a mutual attraction between himself and a female patient. He had thought of referring her to the therapist. At this point, his female partner interjected to the therapist: "Funnily enough, the last time that happened to me was with Mr G. In fact, I actually considered inviting him on holiday with me, but I decided to refer him to you instead"!'

It is not only between professional colleagues, however, that unconscious conflict produces ambivalent behaviour. As is well known, the doctor also has to deal with his own emotional reactions to patients, which may unconsciously influence clinical care; witness the following example:

'A GP began to tell a therapist about one of his patients, who was a longstanding hypochondriac. The patient had returned to the surgery with multiple complaints over many years, and the GP felt at a loss to know how to cure her. She began to complain of chronic constipation, and the GP examined her and found that there was no constipation. He therefore concluded that the patient was suffering from an hypochondriacal delusion. But the patient insisted on being referred to a surgeon and so the GP, against his better judgement, agreed. To his amazement, the surgeon suggested doing an ileostomy. The GP felt that this treatment was completely wrong, but was also reluctant to discuss the matter with the surgeon and suggest a different course of action. The ileostomy was duly carried out, but the patient then continued to attend the surgery just as regularly with problems connected with her ileostomy, which she had nick-named "Cyril".'

It seemed that the GP here felt guilty about having referred the patient for what he now saw as punishment. The patient herself seemed unperturbed by the operation, and continued her essentially sado-masochistic relationship with the doctor on the same basis as before.

THE MIDDLE PERIOD

It is sometimes implied that simply by working more closely with GPs, better communication can be achieved. However, this view seems optimistically naive in regard to the unconscious roots of many of the failures in communication which inevitably occur. Close working relationships can, on occasion, result in worse communications.

The pressure of work in general practice leads to an atmosphere of hurry and busy activity. Time is at a premium and conversations about patients are often squeezed into the minutes between surgeries, whilst standing in the corridor. With personal access to a consultant, these hurried conversations may be substituted for the often more thoughtful formulations which are encouraged by the process of writing a traditional referral letter. It is well known that patients may spend a long time in consultation with their doctor, only to reveal their deepest worry as they get up to leave the room. In like manner, severe anxieties which may be worrying the doctor are not always ventilated at close quarters, and may be lightly dismissed or given second place to the most trivial of activities, as the following vignette indicates:

'A therapist was invited to lunch in a general practice, which was regularly provided by a drug company. The therapist thought that the purpose of the working lunch was to discuss cases, but in fact, most of the time was spent in social chit-chat. At the end of the lunch, the GP took the therapist aside and asked to have a word about a problem. There was a great deal of anxiety that a man would murder his ex-wife. They were living together in the same house – the woman on the top floor and the husband on the lower floor. The GP worried that if he prescribed an anti-depressant, the man would become disinhibited and murder his wife (he apparently knew of another case where this happened). However, the man had demanded treatment for himself, and had threatened to murder his wife if the doctor failed to prescribe. Thus, the GP felt that whatever he did, the man would murder his wife. This serious anxiety was given about two minutes discussion between the end of the lunch and the beginning of the afternoon surgery.'

Hospital doctors sometimes like to think that even if they do not know their individual patients very well, at least the family doctor is in close contact with them. But with the advent of large health centres and group practices, this is not always the case. In one surgery, the following episode occurred:

'A visiting therapist was stopped in the corridor by one of the GPs who told him that he had just seen a patient whom he was worried about. This was a woman in her thirties, who had been in conflict with her mother in the past. The patient had been tearful in her interview with the GP that morning, and he thought she might be depressed. He was in a hurry, and added that he would give the therapist further details later on. In due course, the therapist received a note, explaining that the patient had had a series of abortions in the distant past.

When the therapist saw the patient, she did not say anything about the abortions, even when given the opportunity to do so. Instead, she complained of life-long frigidity, which had prevented her from ever having sexual intercourse! The therapist was becoming somewhat bewildered, and began to feel that she was not revealing the real truth about her problems. After the interview, the therapist told the GP about his experience and the doctor suddenly realised that he had written to the therapist using the notes of a completely different patient, which happened to be on his desk, to remind himself of the woman's history!'

Another failure in communication, in spite of close working arrangements, occurred in the following way:

'A patient was referred to a therapist by a GP, who said that the patient had been complaining of pains without a physical cause and might be depressed. Little else was communicated to the therapist about the patient.

During the first interview, the patient confessed that she was in love with the GP and claimed that she had evidence that her love was reciprocated. She cited the fact that the GP visited her at home at least twice a week and conducted many physical examinations. He sometimes dropped little notes into her letter box, telling her that he had called. She was convinced that it was only the fact that the GP was married that prevented him from openly declaring his love.

Later, the therapist was able to discuss the case briefly with the GP and tried to help the doctor to understand the patient's state of mind, and at the same time set limits to the number of house visits which he made. The GP then confided that he felt blackmailed by the patient, feeling that he had to visit the patient whenever she called, in case he missed diagnosing a serious illness. He knew this patient was of a litigious disposition, and worried about becoming involved in legal actions. The GP was about to go off on a sabbatical, and before he left, he struck the patient off his list. A few weeks later, the therapist received a letter from the patient's solicitor, saying that his client had been making accusations against the GP and the solicitor felt that his client was mentally ill.

The therapist regretted the failure in communication which had left the GP unable to reveal the true nature of the problems he was having; and that, having revealed them, he then felt it necessary to escape completely, rather than accept the support of the therapist.'

This pattern of events is, in fact, not uncommon in general practice. What usually happens is that an enthusiastic GP starts off by giving some regular interviews to a patient who appears to have psychological problems. The GP feels that the patient might benefit from the opportunity to talk things through. An intensely dependent transference relationship soon develops, but the GP is not trained to deal with and understand it. With the passage of time, the GP begins to feel increasingly burdened by the patient's demands, but finds it difficult to reject them, and thus risk becoming a bad object in the patient's eyes. Eventually, the doctor becomes disillusioned with his psychotherapeutic efforts, which appear only to worsen the situation, and he may suddenly reject the patient in an uncharacteristically harsh manner. He will at this point arrange for another partner to take over, or refer the patient to a psychotherapist for treatment, if one is available.

ENDING AN ATTACHMENT

Problems related to dependency and separation can be equally manifest in the relationship between GP and visiting psychotherapist. When the time comes for an attachment to end, any ambivalence which occurred in the early stages may re-emerge, and it is helpful for both parties to be able to recognise this when it happens. Once again, in the following example, the patient's problem is germane to an understanding of the underlying conflict:

'A therapist had been working closely with a general practice for several years, and had become a valued member of the team. As well as seeing patients, she had regular meetings with the GPs to discuss cases.

The therapist obtained a new job in a different town, which meant that she would have to give up her attachment to the practice. She gave the doctors advance notice of her departure, and they expressed their appreciation of her contribution and regrets that she was leaving.

Then about six weeks before the therapist was due to leave, a patient was referred who had an irrational fear that her daughter would die. The therapist wanted to discuss the case at their usual lunch-time meeting, but she was surprised to find that the GPs had unwittingly arranged another meeting at this time. Instead of their usual psychotherapy conference, they had organised a lunch with a drug company to discuss the management of "heart attacks".

The initial irritation which the therapist experienced on hearing this news was soon modified by her understanding of the GPs' difficulty in coming to terms with losing her and of the extent of their emotional involvement in the attachment, illustrated perhaps by the nature of the referred patient's problem and the subject matter of the lunch-time meeting.'

The placement of a mental health professional in a general practice setting may offer the possibility of better communication, but this will develop slowly, and there may be many misunderstandings along the way. The GP and the psychotherapist have different expectations of each other and of their patients. They are used to working in contrasting settings, and the relationship is marred at the outset both by society's reaction in general to psychiatrists and by the possible experiences the GP may already have had, working at a distance from the psychiatrist. The opportunity for better communication certainly exists and should not be allowed to slip away, though it must be recognised that the relationship is going to be unavoidably stressful.

It is exceedingly difficult in the context of general practice for doctors to adopt a frame of mind which allows them to acknowledge their own vulnerability and neediness when, in terms of their patients, they feel they must appear strong and self-reliant. Receiving help in managing psychological problems from a visiting psychotherapist is often felt to be equivalent to entering the patient role, and therefore threatens the doctor's professional identity; it may be seen as a sign of weakness. As a defence against this, the doctor may behave in such a way as to make the therapist feel under-valued. Both partners then feel hurt.

It is not my intention here to devalue attempts at liaison work between mental health professionals and primary health care teams. If I have dwelt upon the difficulties, and selected the conflicts to describe, it is because I want to temper current enthusiasm for the idea with a realistic account of the problems that are likely to be encountered – problems for which there is no easy panacea.

ACKNOWLEDGEMENTS

I am grateful both to the GPs and members of the Ashhurst Team who have participated in the development of the liaison work, particularly Drs M. Whalley and J. Small and Messrs. D. Kennard, D. Jones, D. Fordwour, and I. Stapeley, as well as to Mrs. P. Finlay for secretarial assistance.

10
Multiple Personality

We are inclined to take it for granted that each person has just one body which changes slowly with the passage of time. But the unity of mind or 'soul' has often seemed problematic – something not given, but rather achieved with difficulty. Thus Plato (*Republic*, 443) suggests that work is required in order to integrate the diverse parts of a man's inner self: 'Only when a man has linked these parts together in well-tempered harmony and has made himself one man instead of many, will he be ready to go about whatever he may have to do...' (Kenny 1973).

Inconsistencies in human experience and behaviour may therefore have seemed unremarkable until the notion of a unique unchanging identity, attributable to every man, gained general acceptance. That this should ever have happened requires some explanation. L.L. Whyte puts it nicely when he says:

'The intuitive sense of a persisting experiencing self constitutes a treacherous basis for an ordering of experience, because the direct awareness of the human individual does not justify the attribution to the self either of permanence, or of unchanging identity, or of continuous awareness. Indeed the facts of growth, aging, and death, and the transitory wandering character of awareness render this assumption of a permanent identical conscious subject most peculiar. Why did the human mind ever make such a strange, apparently perverse, "inference"?' (Whyte 1979)

Whyte argues that self-awareness helps man to master his environment and satisfy his needs. In doing so it paradoxically reduces the disjunction between biological need and environmental provision, and thus destroys the basis for its own existence. Self-awareness is basically self-eliminating. Seventeenth century rationalism failed to realise this and 'invented' a single, enduring, cognitive, rational self, which colonised man's identity and gave rise to a peculiarly modern malaise – the pain of unmitigated self-consciousness.

The notion of unconscious mental process, Whyte suggests, acted as a balm for this condition and provided a kind of counterbalance to Descartes' equation of mind with awareness. It was, he writes: '...*conceivable* (in post-Cartesian Europe) around 1700, *topical* around 1800, and *fashionable* around 1870–1880'.

Accordingly throughout this period, interest in the discontinuities of human experience – altered states of consciousness, dreams, somnambulism, and automatism, – the outer manifestations of a contradictory and hidden inner process, continued to grow.

EARLY CASE-REPORTS

Cases of abrupt changes in personality accompanied by disturbances in awareness have been reported for at least two hundred years. One of the earliest examples dates from 1789. A young German woman, impressed by the arrival in Stuttgart of aristocratic refugees from the French Revolution, suddenly 'exchanged' her own personality for the manners and ways of a French-born lady, speaking French fluently and German as would a French woman. Eberhardt Gmelin, who published the case, was apparently able with a wave of his hand, to induce repeated changes between 'French' and 'German' states. In her French personality, the young woman had complete memory of all that she had said and done during her previous French states, but as a German she knew nothing of her French personality! (Ellenberger 1970).

Another famous case, that of a young English woman called Mary Reynolds, was first published in 1816 by Dr. John Kearsley Mitchell. She oscillated between two different personality states over a period of fifteen or sixteen years, finally settling in the second state until her death in 1854 at the age of 69. In her first state she was quiet, sober and thoughtful with a tendency to depression, whilst in her second state she was gay, cheerful, extravagant, fond of company and practical jokes, with a strong propensity for versification and rhyming.

Joseph Breuer's patient, Anna O (Breuer and Freud 1893–95), sometimes credited with the birth of psychoanalysis (as well as a pseudocyesis that embarrassed her physician), also demonstrated a double personality. When Breuer took over her treatment in December 1880, she manifested two entirely distinct states of consciousness which alternated frequently and without warning. In one she recognised her surroundings, was melancholy and anxious, but relatively normal. In the other she hallucinated and was 'naughty' – throwing cushions at people, tearing buttons from her bedclothes and producing numerous defects of speech and language. At one stage she apparently spoke only in English to the consternation of those around her. Later, after the death of her father in April 1881 a new feature of her 'condition seconde' developed – she appeared to be living in the Winter of the preceding year. Breuer was easily able to induce a change of state by holding an orange before her eyes. She coined the terms 'talking cure' and 'chimney sweeping' to describe the hypnotic procedure whereby, through tracing the circumstances in which her symptoms originated, she was able to gain relief.

In 1886 a Dr. Myers summarised the case of a male patient known as Louis V (*Science*, 1886) who was said to have six different states of consciousness, all of them more or less accompanied by distinct physical conditions, and different types of amnesia. The application of soft iron to his right thigh apparently restored most of his memory and temporarily dispelled all paralysis. Under other magnetic conditions, a sudden change of character occurred whereby, from being 'arrogant, violent, and profane, with indistinct utterance and complete inability to write'; he became 'quiet, modest, and respectful, speaking easily and clearly and able to write with a fair hand', though the greater part of his life remained a blank to him.

Ellenberger goes so far as to suggest that the entire nineteenth century was preoccupied with the problems that magnetism and hypnotism threw up regarding the constitution of the human mind. After the turn of the century most cases were reported as having more than two personalities. (Prince 1920). Dipsychism a dualistic concept, gave way to polypsychism, which saw the mind as a cluster of subpersonalities and finds its modern expression in psychoanalytic object-relations theory. Dr. Henry Jekyll summarises the position well in Stevenson's famous novella:

> 'I thus drew steadily nearer to that truth by whose partial discovery I have been doomed to such a dreadful shipwreck: that man is not truly one, but truly two. I say two, because the state of my own knowledge does not pass beyond that point. Others will follow, others will outstrip me on the same lines; and I hazard the guess that man will be ultimately known for a mere polity of multifarious, incongruous and independent denizens.' (Stevenson 1886)

NOSOLOGICAL STATUS

The place of multiple personality phenomena in a classification of mental disorders, is by no means settled. Several positions, not all mutually exclusive, need to be considered:

(1) *Multiple personality represents the normal but frequently unacknowledged condition of mankind. Hence it is a problem for grammar rather than medicine* (Tantam 1990). This position fails to take account of the arresting fascination of case reports over two centuries. Mundane happenings do not normally stimulate such interest. The argument is easier to sustain in its weaker form – that multiple personality differs only in degree and not in kind from normal psychology. Freud adopted this view when he wrote the following lines, though he may have been over

sanguine in thinking the concept of 'identification' was explanatory
rather than merely descriptive:

> 'perhaps the secret of the cases of what is described as "multiple
> personality" is that the different identifications seize hold of
> consciousness in turn. Even when things do not go so far as this,
> there remains the question of conflicts between the various
> identifications into which the ego comes apart, conflicts which
> cannot after all be described as entirely pathological. (Freud 1923)

(2) *Multiple personality is a factitious entity constructed by malingerers, or naively
    generated with iatrogenic help!* Illness confers alterations in social status,
    most notably release from normal social obligations, and possible legal
    defences against criminal charges (albeit with the simultaneous
    imposition of an alternative role). It may therefore be simulated for
    social gain. Professionals may be inclined to make diagnoses for the
    same reason, or because a given condition has become officially
    recognised or fashionable! Hypnotic suggestion might also encourage
    the manufacture of new identities. (Chodoff 1987). Such factors may
    explain the 'epidemic' of case reports emanating from North America
    over the last twenty years. (Boor 1982; Merskey 1992). Sceptics,
    however, must explain those cases which seem to arise spontaneously,
    outside any legal context, and those (possibly as large a proportion as
    90%) where dissimulation appears to have been attempted. (Kluft
    1987a). There is a body of opinion which holds that it is impossible
    for a person to consistently fake multiplex cognitive, affective and
    behavioural patterns over an extended period of time. (Watkins 1984;
    Orne *et al.* 1984; Kluft 1987b).

(3) *Multiple personality is a mental disorder* sui generis. This is the present
    orthodoxy expounded in DSM-III and DSM-III-R (American
    Psychiatric Association 1980, 1987), where it is classified under the
    general rubric of dissociative disorders, and in ICD-10 (World Health
    Organisation 1992). In DSM-III, two or more distinct personalities (or
    personality states) are required to exist in the same person. A second
    criterion insists that the person's behaviour must be 'fully controlled' at
    different times by more than one of these personalities. The disorder is
    said to originate in childhood almost invariably, where there is
    frequently a history of physical and sexual abuse. More than one
    hundred personalities may occur, with varying degrees of awareness
    and memory of each other. Transition between them is often sudden.

The presence of amnesia between the 'primary personality' and others, has been held to be important in eliminating false-positive diagnoses.

A personality is defined as: 'a relatively enduring pattern of perceiving, relating to, and thinking about the environment and one's self that is exhibited in a wide range of important social and personal contexts'; personality states differ only in that they exhibit themselves in a narrower band of situations. Among the associated features, it is claimed that various personalities in the same person may have different physiological characteristics e.g. skin-resistance, rate of vital functions, brain blood flow, EEG and visual acuity. They may also score differently on IQ tests, respond differently to pharmacological preparations and report themselves to be of different sex, age or race, displaying supposedly characteristic behaviours.

Clearly, this definition introduces a controversial principle into the diagnostic process, in so far as it institutionalises the notion that human behaviour may be controlled not by individual persons but by a plurality of 'personalities' which inhabit persons. Thus the diagnosis of Multiple Personality Disorder, according to the DSM-III, automatically commits the diagnostician to an opinion which undermines the notion of individual autonomy. This, as we shall see, leads to extraordinary difficulties in assessing criminal responsibility, and is, to say the least, an unverifiable assumption. If the law is to avoid tautology, the existence of mental disorder giving rise to impaired responsibility, must surely be established on other independent grounds.

(4) *Multiple personality is a symptom characteristic of a range of psychological disturbances.* These include hysteria, borderline personality disorder, affective and schizophrenic states and epileptic conditions. This is close to the position taken by DSM-II (American Psychiatric Association 1968) and the conclusion felt to be most consistent with available evidence by Fahy (1988), after an extensive review of the literature. It is more satisfactory (though some might say shirks the issue) because it is fundamentally agnostic. Recognition and description of 'the symptom' does not entail commitment to a particular diagnosis, aetiological theory, treatment regime or untenable moral philosophy. Each case can be assessed on its merits, leaving the question of 'responsibility for the control of behaviour' out of the diagnostic criteria, for some transcendent legal or divine authority to decide!

FORENSIC IMPLICATIONS

In modern times, one of the inherent assumptions in a society regulated by the Rule of Law, is the general recognition of the principle that responsibility is personal and individual (Lloyd 1964). Individuals are accorded both rights and duties, and are only to be answerable for their own wrongdoing. The notion of individual moral responsibility may be an unjustifiable and unassessable meta-physical construct, yet the wellbeing of society seems to require it.

The putative existence of multiple identities in one body has far-fetched social consequences, and challenges assumptions which we normally take for granted. Is, for example, each identity to be awarded a separate vote? Does punishment of one identity offend against the principle that there should be no vicarious liability, if other 'innocent' identities must suffer along with the guilty one? Can a guilty identity escape justice by 'hiding' behind an innocent one? Can multiple identities give testimony to prove a felony?

The case of Kenneth Bianchi (The Los Angeles 'Hillside Strangler') is one in point. During the autumn and winter of 1977–78, the naked bodies of 10 women who had been raped and then strangled were found on various hillsides of Los Angeles County. In January 1979, two further victims were found in a vacant house in Bellingham, Washington, and physical evidence led to the arrest of Bianchi. After interrogation, the Los Angeles police did not consider Bianchi to be a likely suspect for the killings in their area.

Bianchi gave his defence attorney an alibi which was grossly at variance with the facts. When faced with this, he claimed to have invented the story in order to fill in gaps in his memory. His claim of amnesia led the defence to call in a forensic hypnotist, who elicited an alter-personality, 'Steve', apparently unknown to Ken, claiming responsibility for the two local killings and nine of the ten Los Angeles deaths. John Watkins, the hypnotist, found Bianchi to be 'a pleasant, mild young man who seemed to be earnestly seeking to understand what had happened and why he was in jail', and who at no time showed any concern for his legal fate. (Watkins 1984).

'Steve', however, when seen by another investigator out of trance, was described as 'very crude and nasty, using the word "fuck" in every sentence, and claiming to have committed the crime to get Ken out of the way, so that he could control the body full-time.' (Allison 1984). In an attempt to discover whether Bianchi was malingering, it was suggested to him (in his normal state) that real cases of multiple personality invariably had at least three personalities. Under hypnosis a third personality,'Billy', duly emerged, and this, together with other inconsistencies led prosecution witnesses to conclude that the correct diagnosis was Antisocial Personality Disorder with Sexual Sadism.

This split in expert opinion eventually resulted in a plea bargain, in which Bianchi pleaded guilty (avoiding the death penalty) and was sentenced to several terms of life imprisonment. Nevertheless, professional controversy regarding his diagnosis, and the means by which 'true' cases of multiple personality can be distinguished, continues unabated. It should be noted that at no stage in this case was the validity of multiple personality disorder *per se*, called into question by the expert witnesses, though it has subsequently been suggested by one of them that determining the correct diagnosis in a death penalty case, may be an impossible task (Allison 1984).

Another case, under trial in Wisconsin at the time of writing, and reported in *The Times* (London), highlights the legal conundrums that the diagnosis engenders. Here the crime is said to have been made possible as a result of the victim's multiple personality!

> 'Mark Peterson, a shop assistant, aged 29, is accused of raping Sarah by summoning "Jennifer", a "20-year-old who likes to dance and have fun", and having sex with her in his car. During intercourse, a six-year-old personality known as Emily intruded. She told Sarah, who subsequently telephoned the police to report that she had been assaulted. On Wednesday the prosecutor and judge patiently questioned Sarah before "summoning" and separately swearing in "Jennifer" and "Franny", a "30-year-old".' (*The Times* 1990)

CLINICAL ISSUES

From the psychodynamic point of view, multiple personality is regarded as a defence against anxiety, originally experienced in infancy. It has been suggested that the 'split' involved is in the ego, rather than between the ego and the id. (Marmer 1980). Object-relations language sees it both in the 'self' and its 'internal objects', or their 'representations'. The high prevalence of adverse childhood experiences reported in these patients is consistent with this, very general, hypothesis.

Another way of seeing this defence invokes the notion of 'self-hypnosis' (Bliss 1980). Hypnosis is here regarded as a phylogenetically old CNS mechanism for protecting animals from danger. As a third alternative to fight and flight, self-hypnosis may produce physiological changes that allow the animal to remain immobile and 'freeze' for extended periods of time. In man this mechanism may lead to an altered state of consciousness whereby unpleasant experiences are forgotten or allocated out of awareness to alternative personalities. Most often discovered in childhood, it is suggested that in cases of multiple personality it thereafter develops into a primary method for coping with stress.

Information from split brain observations also provides a biological model. Thus it is clear that when the corpus callosum is severed a man may engage in bewilderingly contradictory behaviour. In one case a husband embraced his wife with one hand and pushed her away with the other. A second person's right and left hand chose different clothes to wear. (Sperry 1965). These findings together with the evidence of altered brain physiology in some cases, raise the possibility of an underlying biological basis for the dissociative states.

However we look at multiple personality, there can be no doubt that people present to psychiatric services requiring help for this condition, and some workers feel it is insufficiently recognised (Ross 1987). A wide range of therapeutic strategies has been tried, singly and in combination, including drugs, ECT, hypnosis and various forms of psychotherapy (Herzog 1984; Ross and Gahan 1984).

On the whole these people are difficult to help, and in addition to personality change frequently manifest depression, suicide attempts, substance abuse, amnesia, fugue, auditory hallucinations and headaches (Coons and Milstein 1986). Hysterical conversion symptoms such as numbness, blindness, weakness and convulsions are also often reported. Even experienced therapists who take on such patients, find the work tedious and time consuming, and are prone to feel angry, exasperated and emotionally exhausted by the task (Coons 1986).

In inpatient settings physical restraint is required and sessions are frequently begun 'in the seclusion room, knowing that angry, abusive alters are likely to be out of control when called out. Often orderlies are on standby outside the room.' (Ross 1987).

Apart from treating any underlying condition, therapeutic efforts are usually aimed at effecting 'integration' in the patient, for which Kluft has proposed six criteria:

(1) continuity of memory

(2) absence of dissociation

(3) subjective sense of unity

(4) absence of alter personalities under hypnosis

(5) modification of the transference consistent with fusion

(6) presence of previously segregated feelings, attitudes and memories in the fused personality.

This may come about swiftly (in eight outpatient sessions; Ross 1987) or require prolonged psychotherapy lasting more than ten years.

In the absence of controlled studies the efficacy of treatment is difficult to evaluate. What follow-up information there is, does not give grounds for excessive optimism. Kluft's extensive outcome study over a period of ten years revealed only fifteen per cent of 161 treated patients to be integrated (Kluft 1985), while

Coons found three quarters of twenty patients to have remained unintegrated after a variable period of time (Coons 1986). Antipsychotic medication appeared generally unhelpful in this group, but tricyclic antidepressants were judged effective in three of six patients. In a single case study, carbamazepine has also been reported to be useful in the control of dissociation and violent episodes (Fichter *et al.* 1990). Nevertheless it must be conceded, that there is no unequivocal evidence to show that multiple personality is susceptible to anything other than spontaneous change.

11

Hans Andersen's Nightingale
A Paradigm for the Development of Transference Love

I want to look at Hans Andersen's fairy tale *The Nightingale* for the sake of the light which it casts on a person's relationship with his internal objects. The movement which happens in the relationship between the Emperor and the nightingale in the story is also, I think, a paradigm for the natural history of the transference as it seems to unfold in Kleinian analysis. I'll give you a précis of the tale and then make some comments.

THE NIGHTINGALE

A Chinese Emperor lived in the finest palace of the world, which was made entirely of porcelain. One day, while reading a book written by a visitor who had passed through his garden, he was surprised to find a reference to the nightingale as the best thing of all in his empire. The Emperor seemed to feel annoyed and hurt by his ignorance, declaring, 'The whole world knows what I possess – and I know nothing!' He commanded his courtiers to find the bird immediately and bring it to him. Following the directions of a lowly kitchen maid the bird was eventually found and agreed to sing in the Emperor's palace.

After her first performance which was a great hit, it was arranged that she be kept at court in a special cage. Twelve attendants were assigned to her, each of whom held a silk ribbon fastened around her leg, and she was allowed out twice a day for exercise. Soon afterwards the Emperor received a gift from the Emperor of Japan. It was a clockwork nightingale encrusted with jewels. Around its neck it carried the motto, 'The Emperor of Japan's nightingale is poor beside the Emperor of China's'. Nevertheless, everybody at court became entranced by the artificial bird, which was said to keep perfect time and to follow exactly the methods of the Master of the Emperor's Music. During a solo performance given by the artificial bird, in which she repeated the same song thirty-three times, the real nightingale flew out of the window and escaped to her own green woods. The Emperor became alarmed when he noticed that the nightingale had gone. His courtiers immediately accused the nightingale of ingratitude, at the same time asserting that the artificial bird was in any case far superior, being a wonderful model of the human mind at work. It was entirely predictable and its mechanism could be fully understood in terms of causal relationships. The real nightingale was banished from the land and the clockwork nightingale was promoted to a high position by the Emperor's bedside. Because people could easily imitate the sound of the clockwork bird and join in, they grew to like it even more. Then, after a year, the artificial bird suddenly broke. Difficulties in repair meant that now it would be able to sing only once a year.

Subsequently, the Emperor fell sick. He was thought unlikely to live and a successor was chosen. As he lay on his bed he felt Death sit on his chest and remove his crown and imperial regalia. The Emperor's good and evil deeds in the form of strange faces, both hideous and kind, peered at him from the folds in the curtains, reminding him of his past and continuously asking him if he remembered this or that. At length the Emperor cried out in anguish, imploring the artificial nightingale to sing in order to blot out the sound of the voices. But the bird did not respond. It could not sing because there was no one to wind it up.

A moment later the voice of the real nightingale, singing the Emperor consolation and hope, burst through the window. Death himself was captivated and forced to yield up the Emperor's possessions in order to persuade the bird to go on singing. The Emperor grew stronger and was filled with gratitude towards the nightingale, asking how he could ever repay her, but the bird required nothing more than the tears of appreciation which came into his eyes as she sang.

The Emperor now wished to keep the nightingale close to him for ever and determined to destroy the artificial bird. But the nightingale protested, arguing that the artificial bird had done her best. The nightingale then declared that she was unable to make her home in the palace because she had to fly around to the distant homes of other people – poor fishermen and humble peasants – but she promised to come when she felt she wanted to. Finally she made the Emperor promise one thing – that he would not let anybody know that he had a little bird who told him everything. Then she flew away. When the Emperor's servants entered the room expecting to find him dead, they were confronted with a live and healthy Emperor.

COMMENTS

It seems to me that in this story the palace and the garden, together with all the people and objects they contain, can be taken to represent the internal world of the Emperor. The Emperor himself could then represent the ego, and the story could be seen as tracing the development of the ego and describing the progress and quality of its object relations.

Initially then, I think it is interesting to note that the Emperor lives in the finest palace in the world, but this palace is made of porcelain and therefore easily shattered. One could say that the Emperor feels himself to be inside his object, which is at the same time idealised and fragile. The Emperor's identification also has an artificial and obtrusive quality about it. Thus, in the story, the loveliest flowers in his garden have silver bells tied onto them in order to ensure that they are noticed.

The theme is repeated when the Emperor's sycophantic courtiers, immediately after hearing the bird sing, foolishly think that they too can be nightingales and fill their mouths up with water in order to be able to gurgle when anyone speaks to them. Later on in the story, the qualities of the real nightingale are denied altogether and the artificial bird becomes exalted but soon breaks down. This kind of idealisation of the self could represent a manic defence mediated by the mechanism of projective identification. This defence, described by Melanie Klein (1935), is characterised by a denial of psychic reality. The ego denies the importance of its good objects and ignores the threats posed by its bad objects and the id. The sense of omnipotence is utilised for the purpose of gaining mastery and control over these objects. In the same paper Klein describes the anxieties giving rise to this defence, thus:

> 'I would suggest that in mania the ego seeks refuge not only from melancholia but also from a paranoiac condition which it is unable to master. Its torturing and perilous dependence on its loved objects drives the ego to find freedom. But its identification with these objects is too profound to be renounced. On the other hand, the ego is pursued by its dread of bad objects and of the id and, in its effort to escape from all these miseries, it has recourse to many different mechanisms...' (p.277)

In the mechanism of projective identification a subject may intrude into an object, take possession of it and thus acquire a pseudo-identity (Klein 1955b). In spite of the apparent superiority of the pseudo-identity thus formed, it remains in fact weak and easily damaged. The story seems to be saying that splitting, denial and manic projective identification are unsatisfactory methods for building a strong character.

In contrast to the Emperor, the nightingale lives in a place far away from the centre of attention. She inhabits a glorious wood with tall trees and deep lakes going down to the sea which allow big ships to sail right in under the branches. She is celebrated by poor fishermen and travelling poets. An allusion to genital intercourse can be clearly drawn and supports the idea that the nightingale as a good object is somehow connected with or perhaps produced as a result of sexual love.

At the beginning of the story the Emperor is isolated from his good object – the nightingale – to the extent that he is completely unaware of its existence. In place of dependence on a good object he is supported by a Court of flatterers over whom he exercises tyrannical control. The quality of his object relations is spelled out when after first reading about the bird, he petulantly commands his gentleman-in-waiting to find her immediately.

This 'gentleman' is an object who placates and soothes the Emperor with false information. When he cannot find the nightingale he tells the Emperor that she must be a figment of the writer's imagination, a product of black art. But the Emperor now has his heart set on finding the nightingale and threatens to punch all his courtiers in the stomach if the bird is not found!

In this state of mind the Emperor receives little genuine help from his objects but rather has an unholy alliance with them to distort reality and bolster his own sense of power. It takes somebody else, represented in the story by a visitor or lowly kitchen maid, to recognise his good object and bring him into contact with it. This could be taken to be the function of the psychoanalyst in the analytical situation. The kitchen maid seems to be in a fundamentally depressive relationship with the nightingale but the Emperor is not. In the story the maid brings scraps from the Emperor's table to her poor sick mother and stops on her way to hear the bird singing, which brings tears to her eyes just as if her mother were kissing her. The Emperor, however, wishing to exert omnipotent control over the nightingale, sets out both to patronise and to imprison her. Although he is moved to tears by the nightingale's song, his own insight and appreciation remain superficial. He has, in effect, incorporated the nightingale into his own narcissistic organisation. Thus, when a parcel arrives one day with the word, 'Nightingale' written on the outside the Emperor declares proudly, 'I expect this is a new book written about *our famous* bird' (my italics). He is easily seduced by the pretty, artificial bird into a state of narcissistic self-glorification. While his attention is focused on the false counterpart, the Emperor loses his good object in spite of his attempts to control it and, perhaps as a result of this loss, he eventually becomes ill and nearly dies.

The reaction of his courtiers is to deny altogether the value of the real nightingale. The limitations and predictability of the clockwork bird are elevated into wonderful demonstrations of the workings of the human mind and the variety and creative originality of the nightingale's song is repudiated because of its unpredictable nature.

The 'group' in the form of the general public is mobilised in order to support this attack on the Emperor's good object. The Emperor's Master of Music arranges to show the clockwork bird to the public and the essentially masturbatory nature of this activity seems to be indicated by their reactions: 'they were as delighted as if they had drunk themselves merry on tea ... they all said, "Oh" and held up one finger – the finger we call "lick-pot" – and nodded their heads.'

At first this defensive manoeuvre appears to hold and the Emperor has great fun trying to imitate the clockwork bird, but after a year the machinery snaps. The parts are worn out and the Emperor begins to feel sad when he realises the impossibility of adequately repairing the bird.

With the passage of time he becomes prey to persecutory hallucinations and, perhaps one could say, under the domination of the death instinct. He is particularly tormented by his developing insight and by the things he had never realised before that the voices tell him about. It seems that he is about to be overwhelmed by depressive anxiety. But the nightingale rescues him, returns in the nick of time, disarms death and restores him to health.

Now the Emperor's relationship to his object undergoes an important change. First he is filled with gratitude and a sense of knowing to whom he owes his peace of mind. He wishes to make reparation to the bird and repay his debt. Then he is seized by the need to be constantly near her. This time, of course, he recognises that he cannot control the bird but that he is necessarily dependent upon her.

Furthermore, he is now able to tolerate the knowledge of his evil deeds which were previously experienced as persecutory, for the nightingale says, 'my singing can make you both gay and thoughtful ... I shall sing of the good and the evil that are lurking about you'. In this state of mind the Emperor is able to give his object its freedom, respecting the boundary between himself and the nightingale and yet wishing to be always by her side. One could say that he had reached the depressive position but, of course, the nightingale warned him to keep it a secret. Presumably she may have thought that the Emperor in such a position was vulnerable to group pressure and attacks and that his depressive relationship to her would be best preserved by remaining silent.

CONCLUSION

Hans Andersen's fairy tale *The Nightingale* is regarded as a paradigm for the development of the transference in Kleinian analysis. The tale illuminates the movement between paranoid-schizoid and depressive positions and highlights the meaning of trust in a good object.

Character Development in Daniel Deronda
A Psychoanalytic View

In clinical practice we are often confronted with people who lack a sense of security and well-being. These people may be panicky and frightened and feel faint in certain situations. They may find it difficult to leave their home without experiencing unpleasant sensations. They do not feel at home in the world and may be disturbed by a pervasive sense of impending doom or death; danger from which they cannot escape. We say that these people are anxious.

But why are we not all like this? It might be argued that such people are simply opening their eyes to the realities of the human condition. Life is short, we are all dreadfully vulnerable to illness and natural disasters, nations are cruel, fate is harsh and individuals are selfish and violent. On this view the best that we could hope for would be lucky chances in the natural world and kindliness based on some form of enlightened self-interest in those who were stronger than us. Altruism would not exist.

The experience of living in a world where one is perpetually under siege from persecutory forces may not be conducive to the development of qualities of character such as generosity, tolerance, kindliness, and sensitivity to the needs of others; and yet we are confronted with a second observation – not everybody reacts to their human predicament in the same way. In the worst external conditions, in concentration camps and refugee camps, in prisons, in extremis we recognise the existence of acts of courage, heroism, self-sacrifice and love. We never tire of listening to or telling such stories, and we celebrate the existence of these qualities of character in books, plays and films.

So the psychological world in which a person lives need not be totally constrained by the limitations of his physical and social surroundings. It is built up, constructed and re-constructed within the mind, and as a result of the contact of one mind with another. How then is it possible for a person to develop a sense of security and well-being? How possible for destructive impulses to be overcome and for goodness and generosity to exist?

George Eliot was very much concerned with such questions and I want to take some examples from her work. In the opening paragraph of her last novel

Daniel Deronda she touches immediately upon the struggle between good and evil in her description of the heroine Gwendolen Harleth:

> 'Was she beautiful or not beautiful? and what was the secret of form or expression which gave the dynamic quality of her glance? Was the good or the evil genius dominant in those beams? Probably the evil; else why was the effect that of unrest rather than of undisturbed charm? why was the wish to look again felt as coercion and not as a longing in which the whole being consents?' (p.35)

It has been suggested by F. R. Leavis (1948), that Deronda should be considered as two books – a poor one about Daniel Deronda and a great one which ought to be entitled 'Gwendolen Harleth'. This is because, to Leavis, Deronda's character is idealised, schematically drawn and unconvincing, whereas Gwendolen Harleth is a truly tragic figure; a human being in conflict and the only character in the novel to undergo any significant moral development.

She is portrayed at the beginning of the book as a 'spoiled child' who is incapable of love; at the end she is a mature woman whose capacity for love has grown through experiencing grief and remorse. At first however she is aloof, superior and fond of getting her own way.

As we have already heard, her effect on an observer is coercive and disturbing. Her beauty, intelligence and accomplishments seem to ensure that she will gain omnipotent control over all her admirers and she confidently looks forward to exerting this control over any future husband in the same way that she dominates her mother and sisters.

We are told that she was her mother's favourite and that they always slept in the same room. Yet when her mother was in pain at night and asked her to go and get some medicine she 'grumbled and refused'. The following day she 'tried to make amends by caresses that cost her no effort'. Her nature we are told was not remorseless, but she liked to make her penances easy! Nevertheless she suffered from a number of symptoms. She was afraid to be alone at night and suffered occasionally during the day from experiences which were like brief periods of madness, when she was overcome by helpless fear and terror. Here is a description of one of these episodes:

> '... She looked like a statue into which a soul of Fear had entered: her pallid lips were parted; her eyes, usually narrowed under their long lashes, were dilated and fixed. Her mother less surprised than alarmed, rushed towards her, and Rex too could not help going to her side. But the touch of her mother's arm had the effect of an electric charge; Gwendolen fell on her knees and put her hands before her face. She was still trembling, but mute, and it seemed that she had self consciousness enough to aim at controlling her signs of terror ....' (p.92)

Nowadays no doubt she would be diagnosed as suffering from panic attacks and treated by her general practitioner with minor tranquillisers. But we may ask what clues George Eliot has given us as to the origin of Gwendolen's insecurity? Much of psychoanalytical thinking is adumbrated in *Daniel Deronda*. Like Freud, Eliot provides us with a rich variety of metaphor for mental processes. She gives us a 'topographical' model of the mind as a house with unexplored rooms. Thus she describes Rex as:

'a bright, healthy, loving nature, enjoying ordinary innocent things so much that vice had no temptation for him, and what he knew of it lay too entirely in the outer courts and little-visited chambers of his mind for him to think of it with great repulsion.' (p.86)

And again she says of the Meyricks later on:

'their minds being like medieval houses with unexpected recesses and openings from this into that, flights of steps and sudden outlooks.' (p.237)

She is feeling her way towards a concept of the unconscious[1] and is only too aware of the extent to which our behaviour is inexplicable by a psychology which addresses itself to rational motives alone. When Gwendolen suddenly decides not to sell her necklace, George Eliot comments:

'why she should suddenly determine not to part with this necklace was not much clearer to her than why she should sometimes have been frightened to find herself in the fields alone; It was something vague and yet mastering, which impelled her to this action about the necklace. There is a great deal of unmapped country within us which would have to be taken into account in an explanation of our gusts and storms.' (p.321)

She refers to the 'dark seed-growths of consciousness' (p.337) where new wishes form themselves, and like Freud emphasises both 'economic' and 'dynamic' aspects; she presents us with an energetic as well as a hermeneutic analysis (Ricoeur 1970). This is illustrated in her description of Grandcourt (p.194) whose passions were said to be of the intermittent flickering kind: never flaming out strongly. Yet he achieved a good appearance in society 'at a small expense of vital energy' and even his sudden impulses which had a false air of demonic strength may have arisen as the result of:

'the want of regulated channels for the soul to move in – good and sufficient ducts of habit without which our nature easily turns to a mere ooze and mud, and at any pressure yields nothing but a spurt or a puddle.' (p.194).

---

1   Whyte (1979) says 'The general conception of unconscious mental processes was *conceivable* (in post-Cartesian Europe) around 1700, *topical* around 1800, and *fashionable* around 1870–1880' (p.63). It is interesting to note that *Deronda* was published in 1876 during the middle of this period.

Again in accord with psychoanalytical thinking Eliot sees the main lines of character as being laid down in childhood experiences (p.210) which are in turn influenced by innate factors. Thus in Deronda's case we are told that the doubt surrounding his paternity and the possibility that others knew something to his disadvantage, which had been withheld from him, might have led him into 'a hard proud antagonism' had it not been for 'inborn lovingness', which was 'strong enough to keep itself level with resentment' (p.211).

Gwendolen, however, although not totally devoid of potential for goodness, is portrayed as being distinctly lacking in this quality. In her case it is 'inborn energy of egoistic desire' (p.71)[2] which Eliot suspects is the significant factor. A condition which she tells us normally goes hand in hand with a delight in imagining the envy of others (p.323).

Indeed so great is Gwendolen's destructive narcissism and intolerance to frustration that she is said to have murdered her sister's canary, by strangling it in a fit of exasperation, when its singing jarringly interrupted her own (p.53). The anxiety caused to Gwendolen by her murderous impulses;[3] and the attempt to undo their effects symbolically, over and over again, is given expression in her attitude to insects. We are told that she delighted to rescue them from drowning and then watch their recovery (p.53).

But Gwendolen's struggle and longstanding failure to 'resuscitate her mother's mental life' may be gauged from the following passage:

"'Oh yes," said Gwendolen, leaning her head against her mother, though speaking as lightly as she could. "But you know I am never ill. I am as strong as possible; and you must not take to fretting about me, but make yourself as happy as you can with the girls. They are better children to you than I have been, you know." She turned up her face with a smile.

"You have always been good, my darling. I remember nothing else."

"Why, what did I ever do that was good to you, except marry Mr. Grandcourt?" said Gwendolen, starting up with a desperate resolve to be playful, and keep no more on the perilous edge of agitation. "And I should

---

2 Eliot's juxtaposition of the two inborn forces brings to mind the conflict between Freud's (1970) 'Libidinal instinct' and 'ego-instincts'.

3 The preoccupation with murderous impulses and their relation to the death of both internal and external objects is a theme which runs through George Eliot's work. In her first book *Scenes of Clerical Life* in 'Mr. Gilfil's Love Story' the heroine takes up a knife with which she means to murder only to discover when she arrives at the appointed meeting place that her victim has already died of a 'heart attack'. In *Middlemarch*, Madame Laure stabs her husband to death on the stage, 'by mistake' while they are portraying a melodrama. Later she confesses to Lydgate that she had meant to kill him. In her last novel, *Deronda*, a similar ambiguity surrounds the death of Grandcourt by drowning just at the moment when Gwendolen is feeling most murderous towards him.

not have done *that* unless it has pleased myself." She tossed up her chin, and reached her hat.

"God forbid, child! I would not have had you marry for my sake. Your happiness by itself is half mine."

"Very well," said Gwendolen, arranging her hat fastidiously, "then you will please to consider that you are half happy, which is more than I am used to seeing you".' (p.614)

Although she is socially confident and thinks herself well equipped for the mastery of life, her sense of well-being is superficial and precarious. Eliot makes us see that she was in fact ill-equipped to combat the hardships of her early childhood. Not only did she lose her father (who died by an accident in her infancy), but her mother appears to have been a chronically depressed and hypochondriacal character (pp.764, 614, 319). Added to this she had an insecure home background, moving around from one place to another while her step-father, Captain Davilow, joined his family only in a brief and fitful manner.

Listen to how George Eliot describes what Gwendolen lacked:

'Pity that Offendene was not the home of Miss Harleth's childhood, or endeared to her by family memories! A human life, I think, should be well rooted in some spot of a native land, where it may get the love of tender kinship for the face of the earth ... A spot where the definiteness of early memories may be inwrought with affection and kindly acquaintance with all neighbours, even to the dogs and the donkeys, may spread not by sentimental effort and reflection, but as a sweet habit of the blood.' (p.50)

Clearly Eliot is suggesting here that the internalisation of early experiences which are loving and consistent creates the potentiality for the generalisation and spreading of goodwill in a natural way, without any conscious effort or striving on the part of the individual. But does she think it is simply a question of not moving house too often during a child's infancy, or is there more to it than that? What is the first or prototypical experience of security and love? In the same paragraph George Eliot enlightens us:

'At five years old mortals are not prepared to be citizens of the world, to be stimulated by abstract nouns, to soar above preference into impartiality; *and that prejudice in favour of milk with which we blindly begin, is a type of the way body and soul must get nourished at least for a time.*' [my italics] (p.50)

In other words she seems to be saying that the infant's very concrete relationship with the feeding breast precedes the development of symbolic communication and forms the core of the first internalised or *inwrought* sense of affection and goodness.

When this is deficient, as in Gwendolen, a premature denial of dependence sets in which produces a hardening of the self against the possibility of future hurt:

'The perception that poor Rex wanted to be tender made her curl up and harden like a sea-anemone at the touch of a finger.' (p.113)

Signs of vulnerability are eschewed:

'weeping had always been a painful manifestation to be resisted if possible.' (p.335)

A fragile self-sufficiency then asserts that the need for love does not exist, and the capacity to both receive and give love degenerates. this in turn gives rise to a mounting sense of painful emptiness within, and it is when this pain forces itself into consciousness that the hard outer shell of omnipotent denial begins to crack. We can see that soon after Gwendolen rejects Rex's loving advances she breaks down into bitter sobs:

'My child, my child, what is it?' cried the mother, who had never before seen her darling struck down in this way, and felt something of the alarmed anguish that women feel at the sight of overpowering sorrow in a strong man; for this child had been her ruler. Sitting down by her with circling arms, she pressed her cheek against Gwendolen's head, and then tried to draw it upward. Gwendolen gave way, and letting her head rest against her mother, cried out sobbingly, "Oh mamma, what can become of my life? There is nothing worth living for!"

"Why dear?" said Mrs. Davilow. Usually she herself had been rebuked by her daughter for involuntary signs of despair.

"I shall never love anybody. I can't love people. I hate them."

"The time will come, dear, the time will come."

Gwendolen was more and more convulsed with sobbing; but putting her arms round her mother's neck with an almost painful clinging, she said brokenly, 'I can't bear anyone to be very near me but you.'

The mother began to sob, for this spoiled child had never shown such dependence on her before: and so they clung to each other.' (p.115)

Like George Eliot, Melanie Klein felt convinced by experience that the complexity of the fully grown personality could only be understood if we gained insight into the mind of the baby and followed up its development into later life. Let me now quote a passage to you from Klein's book *Envy and Gratitude* (1957) so that you can compare it with George Eliot's writing:

'Throughout my work I have attributed fundamental importance to the infant's first object relation – the relation to the mother's breast and to the mother – and have drawn the conclusion that if this primal object, which is introjected, takes root in the ego with relative security, the basis for a satisfactory development is laid. Innate factors contribute to this bond. Under the dominance of the oral impulse, the breast is instinctively felt to be the source of nourishment and therefore, in a deeper sense, of life itself ...

> The good breast is taken in and becomes part of the ego, and the infant who was first inside the mother now has the mother inside himself.' (pp.178–9)

I think you will agree that they are talking, albeit not with equal eloquence, about the same thing; that the individual's sense of security comes, not simply from his current external circumstances, but from the interplay between these and the quality and level of development of his internal objects.

Perhaps I can reinforce this point now by returning to *Daniel Deronda* and comparing Gwendolen with another character in the book – Mirah. Mirah is a young woman who *did* experience love and trust from her mother in early infancy (p.253). However we are told that her father separated from mother, taking the child Mirah with him from Europe to America. When Mirah wanted to communicate with her mother, father prevented this by telling her that mother was dead! Mirah describes her immediate feeling of desolation but then goes on:

> 'I used to cry every night in my bed for a long while. Then when she came so often to me in my sleep, I thought she must be living about me though I could not always see her, and that comforted me. I was never afraid in the dark, because of that; and very often in the day I used to shut my eyes and bury my face and try to see her and to hear her singing. I came to do that at last without shutting my eyes.' (p.252)

I do not think that we could find a more graphic contrast than the state of mind which Eliot has so beautifully described in these two women; one of whom experiences a panic attack during which the touch of her real mother's arm is experienced like the effect of an electric charge, the other of whom is not frightened of the dark, precisely because she is able to appeal to her good *internal* mother.

However, as Melanie Klein has shown us, the internal world of phantasy is not stable but in a state of continuing flux;

> 'Together with happy experiences, unavoidable grievances reinforce the innate conflict between love and hate, in fact, basically between life and death instincts and result in the feeling that a good and bad breast exist. As a consequence, early emotional life is characterised by a sense of losing and regaining the good object.' (p.180)

Mirah describes clearly how this process may be experienced. She shows that she is closely in touch with the world of psychic reality and how it takes precedence over the exigencies of external reality. She tells us how great is her fear of losing her good internal object when she says:

'... I dreaded doing wrong for I thought I might get wicked and hateful to myself, in the same way that many others seemed hateful to me. For so long, I had never felt my outside world happy; and if I got wicked I should lose my world of happy thoughts where my mother lived with me. That was my childhood notion all through those years. Oh how long they were.' (p.254)

And then how great her despair when the goodness of her internal world finally begins to succumb and she is driven to the point of suicide;

'I did despair. The world seemed miserable and wicked; no one helped me so that I could bear their looks and words; I felt that my mother was dead, and death was the only way up to her.' (p.251)

Nevertheless, because her primal good object had been securely established Mirah is able quickly to retain her sense of goodness when she is rescued by Deronda, for she continues:

'But then in the last moment – yesterday when I longed for the water to close over me – and I thought that death was the best image of mercy – then goodness came to me living, and I felt trust in the living. And – it is strange – but I began to hope that she was living too. And now I am with you – here – this morning, peace and hope have come into me like a flood. I want nothing; I can wait; because I hope and believe and am grateful – oh so grateful! You have not thought evil of me – you have not despised me.' (p.306)

We are given a picture of Mirah's internal world coming back to life, and in the wake of this, trust, hope and gratitude follow.

But what of Gwendolen, whose primal objects we have inferred were not laid down securely. How can we account for the remarkable developments which Eliot describes in her interior world? Certainly they are set in train by the initial check to her omnipotence which is provided by the financial disaster that befalls her family. Finding themselves destitute, the necessity to live on her uncle Gascoigne's charity arises. The acknowledgement of dependence on a 'good object', however, is still unacceptable to Gwendolen's pride, and she experiences it as a humiliation. (p.44)

Her struggles to escape from the dreaded dependent relationship are nevertheless to no avail. First she aspires to 'independence' as an actress and a singer, but this is undermined by Herr Klesmer from whom she seeks advice. He confronts her with the realities of longstanding hard work and discipline that would be necessary to achieve success as an artist, and the probability that she would achieve hardly more than mediocrity (p.305). Gwendolen's fantasies of instantaneous and effortless fame are cruelly dashed and she is forced back into mental conflict.

'For the first time since her consciousness began, she was having a vision of herself on the common level, and had lost the innate sense that there were reasons why she should not be slighted, elbowed, jostled – treated like a passenger with a third-class ticket, in spite of private objections on her own part. She did not move about; the prospects begotten by disappointment were too oppressively preoccupying; she threw herself into the shadiest corner of a settee, and pressed her fingers over her burning eyelids. Every word that Klesmer had said seemed to have been branded into her memory, as most words are which bring with them a new set of impressions and make an epoch for us. Only a few hours before, the dawning smile of self-contentment rested on her lips as she vaguely imagined a future suited to her wishes: it seemed but the affair of a year or so for her to become the most approved Juliet of the time ...' (p.306)

A second solution shortly offers itself to her in the form of marriage to Grandcourt. She is still clinging to her narcissistic hopes and thinks: 'For what could not a woman do when she was married, if she knew how to assert herself?' (p.342). In a last-ditch stand to rescue her sense of superiority, power and control, Gwendolen is impelled towards a union with Grandcourt in spite of her previous promises to Mrs Glasher, whose prior claim upon Grandcourt she fully recognises. Eliot comments prophetically:

'At that moment his strongest wish was to be completely master of this creature – this piquant combination of maidenliness and mischief: that she knew things which had made her start away from him, spurred him to triumph over that repugnance; and he was believing that he should triumph. And she – ah, piteous equality in the need to dominate! – she was overcome like the thirsty one who is drawn towards the seeming water in the desert, overcome by the suffused sense that here in this man's homage to her lay the rescue from helpless subjection to an oppressive lot' (p.346)

Within seven short weeks of marriage we learn that Grandcourt has finally put an end to all Gwendolen's hopes for power and control. This is how Eliot describes it:

'Poor Gwendolen was conscious of an uneasy transforming process – all the old nature shaken to its depths, its hopes spoiled, its pleasures perturbed, but still showing wholeness and strength in the will to reassert itself. After every new shock of humiliation she tried to adjust herself and seize her old supports – proud concealment, trust in new excitements that would make life go by without much thinking; rust in some deed of reparation to nullify her self-blame and shield her from a vague, ever-visiting dread of some horrible calamity; trust in the hardening effect of use and wont that would make her indifferent to her miseries.

Yes – miseries. This beautiful, healthy young creature, with her two-and-twenty years and her gratified ambition, no longer felt inclined to kiss her fortunate image in the glass; she looked at it with wonder that she could be so miserable. One belief which had accompanied her through her un-married life as a self-cajoling superstition, encouraged by the subordination of everyone about her – the belief in her own power of dominating – was utterly gone.' (p.477)

She is thus pushed further into misery and yet at the same time, paradoxically the pre-conditions for her subsequent character development are created. As Henry James put it (1876)

'tragedy *can* have a hold upon her. Her conscience doesn't make the tragedy; that is an old story and, I think a secondary form of suffering. It is the tragedy that makes her conscience, which then reacts upon it; and I can think of nothing more powerful than the way in which the growth of her conscience is traced, nothing more touching than the picture of its helpless maturity.' (p.301)

James's view of the development of conscience is also elaborated by Freud (1924) in his paper 'The economic problem of masochism':

'The situation is usually presented as though ethical requirements were the primary thing and the renunciation of instinct followed from them. This leaves the origin of the ethical sense unexplained. Actually, it seems to be the other way about. The first instinctual renunciation is enforced by external powers, and it is only this which creates the ethical sense, which expresses itself in conscience and demands a further renunciation of instinct.' (p.170)

What seems to happen, is that the renunciation of Gwendolen's impulses towards domination and control, allows the more tender and loving side of her nature to come to the fore. She is then able to form a creatively dependent relationship with Daniel Deronda; a relationship which in the light of psychoanalytic thinking can only be described as *transference love*. It is in the nurturing warmth of this relationship that Gwendolen's capacity to bear remorse gradually grows and along with it her tolerance to separation and mental pain. Without doubt Deronda is able to represent for Gwendolen an object whose capacity for care and concern has been undamaged by envious attacks. His own equanimity and generosity of spirit in the face of being virtually robbed of his inheritance by Grandcourt, is an example to her. Even so, it comes as something of a revelation that such qualities can exist:

'"...– and affection is the broadest basis of good in life."

"Do you think so?" said Gwendolen, with a little surprise. "I should have thought you cared most about ideas, knowledge, wisdom, and all that." But to care about *them* is a sort of affection," said Deronda, smiling at her sudden *naïvete*. "Call it attachment, interest, willingness to bear a great deal for the sake of being with them and saving them from injury. Of course it makes a difference if the objects of interest are human beings; but generally in all deep affections the objects are a mixture – half persons and half ideas – sentiments and affections flow in together!'" (p.470)

But before long she is deeply involved with Deronda who has come to represent an internal object of considerable importance:

'The hidden helplessness gave fresh force to the hold Deronda had from the first taken on her mind, as one who had an unknown standard by which he judged her. Had he some way of looking at things which might be a new footing for her, an inward safeguard against possible events which she dreaded as stored-up retribution? It is one of the secrets in that change of mental poise which has been fitly named conversion, that to many among us neither heaven nor earth has any revelation till some personality touches theirs with a peculiar influence, subduing them into receptiveness. It had been Gwendolen's habit to think of the persons around her as stale books, too familiar to be interesting. Deronda had lit up her attention with a sense of novelty; not by words only, but by imagined facts, his influence had entered into the current of the self-suspicion and self-blame which awakens a new consciousness.

"I wish he could know everything about me without my telling him", was one of her thoughts, as she sat leaning over the end of a couch, supporting her head with her hand and looking at herself in a mirror – not in admiration but in a sad kind of companionship. "I wish he knew that I am not so contemptible as he thinks me – that I am in deep trouble, and want to be something better if I could." Without the aid of sacred ceremony or costume, her feelings had turned this man, only a few years older than herself, into a priest.' (p.509)

Again and again we are made aware of Gwendolen's painful remorse for having injured others (pp.505, 506, 508 ...) and her struggle to be 'good' and to live up to the standards set by her good internal object. She is in conflict, racked now by conscious awareness of her own shortcomings she protests to Deronda about the impossibility of the task before her:

'But if feelings rose – there are some feelings – hatred and anger – how can I be good when they keep rising? And if there came a moment when I felt stifled and could bear it no longer –' (p.509)

We can see however that even under severe pressure from Grandcourt's tyranny and her own murderous anger towards this 'bad' object, she now turns first towards her 'good' object for help; and when she feels Deronda's compassion and senses his pained impotence to intervene on her behalf she becomes suffused with gratitude and exclaims:

> 'I am grieving you. I am ungrateful. You *can* help me. I will think of everything. I will try. Tell me – it will not be a pain to you that I have dared to speak of my trouble to you?...' (p.509)

In the midst of her suffering, Gwendolen's capacity to love is beginning to flower for the first time and in spite of her appalling external circumstances, the state of her internal world is actually improving. The drama which is being played out in her internal world belongs to the phenomenology of what Melanie Klein (1935) called the 'depressive position'. Listen now to how Klein (1955) described the process going on in a child analysis and I think you will be struck by the close correlation with Gwendolen's mental processes.

> 'I have found that the child's attitude towards a toy he has damaged is very revealing. He often puts aside such a toy, representing for instance a sibling or a parent, and ignores it for a time. This indicates dislike of the damaged object, due to the persecutory fear that the attacked person (represented by the toy) has become retaliatory and dangerous. The sense of persecution may be so strong that it covers up feelings of guilt and depression which are also aroused by the damage done. Or guilt and depression may be so strong that they lead to a reinforcing of persecutory feelings. However, one day the child may search in his drawer for the damaged toy. This suggests that by then we have been able to analyse some important defences, thus diminishing persecutory feelings and making it possible for the sense of guilt and the urge to make reparation to be experienced. When this happens we can also notice that a change in the child's relation to the particular sibling for whom the toy stood, or in his relations in general, has occurred. This change confirms our impression that persecutory anxiety has diminished and that, together with the sense of guilt and the wish to make reparation, feelings of love which had been impaired by excessive anxiety have come to the fore. With another child, or with the same child at a later stage of the analysis, guilt and the wish to repair may follow very soon after the act of aggression, and tenderness towards the brother or sister who may have been damaged in phantasy becomes apparent. The importance of such changes for character formation and object relations, as well as for mental stability, cannot be overrated.' (p.128)

Making use of Klein's view then, we may understand the dilemma of the adult Gwendolen as a re-working of the psychological processes which went wrong in her infancy. Her failure to approach the 'depressive position' is now mitigated and through her relationship with Deronda she comes to acknowledge psychic reality and to face squarely the essential and bitter truth:

'that thorn-pressure which must come with the crowning of the sorrowful Better, suffering because of the Worse.' (p.762)

Her internal world has begun to be reconstructed and she is finally ready, as an infant is weaned from the breast, to relinquish her external good object and allow Deronda to leave her and be free. 'Do not think of me sorrowfully on your wedding day', she writes to him 'I have remembered your words – that I may live to be one of the best of women, who make others glad that they were born. I do not yet see how that can be, but you know better than I...' (p.882)

CONCLUSION

I have tried to demonstrate the interplay between internal and external world phenomena in character development by reference to the work of two women. In George Eliot's literary work the theme is brought to life. She affirms the existence of a living and uncharted internal world. Melanie Klein in her psychoanalytical work nearly a century later has helped us to understand it.

13

Destruction and Guilt
Equivocal Death in George Eliot

Psychobiography and its close relative psycho-history have been deservedly criticised in recent years for their tendency to wild speculation, unfounded assertions, and psychological reductionism.[1] Psychoanalysts should be circumspect in their speculations and economical with their claims. Nevertheless the psychoanalytical perspective, with its emphasis on the role of early experience in shaping adult character – an emphasis which George Eliot shared and antedated – and its concept of 'unconscious phantasy', allows us to focus attention on data which are otherwise overlooked. I am far from seeking to explain away George Eliot's genius, nor do I account for the complexity of her art by reference to a single event in her early life. Nothing I say is intended to diminish the importance of appraising socio-cultural factors in her life and work.

No theme occurs more persistently in George Eliot than that of 'equivocal death' – by which I mean the death of a fictional character in circumstances where another is known, or can be inferred, to have wished it. It is present in her first published fiction, *Scenes of Clerical Life* (1858), and spans her literary output. It can be found in her least-known short story, 'The Lifted Veil' (1859), and occurs repeatedly in her most celebrated novel, *Middlemarch* (1871). It endures in *Daniel Deronda* (1876), the last novel to be written before she died in 1880, and is crucial to its development.

Granted that fortuitous death is a conventional literary device in much Victorian fiction, critics and scholars have nevertheless paid insufficient attention to the unique psychological implications of this for George Eliot, and have therefore failed to understand its central significance for her creative drive.[2] I

---

1   See, among others, Michael Shepherd, 'The Psycho-historians', *Encounter,* March 1979, pp.35–42.

2   A notable exception is Carol Christ, 1976, who points out that Eliot repeatedly uses the device of providential death, and suggests that this serves the function of rescuing her characters from aggressive confrontations. Christ thinks that 'a deep prohibition within Eliot herself makes her act against her own stated vision of an indifferent providence', but does not go far in investigating the roots of this prohibition.

Sandra Gilbert (1979), in a feminist critique, *The Madwoman in the Attic*, also draws attention to

believe that her preoccupation with this theme stemmed from an attempt to express and resolve a deep-seated conflict which governed her throughout life.

Where an equivocal death occurs, there is often ambiguity surrounding it – doubt as to the true cause, or questions about motives. This kind of death suggests the possibility not only that a murderous impulse or thought is sufficient to kill the person toward whom it is directed, but that the person who harbours the impulse might also die. Deaths which appear natural or accidental might therefore be murders, and the person with the hostile impulse might then be a murderer and have to bear the consequences – retribution comes swiftly in George Eliot's work. Equally, deaths categorised as murders might turn out to be accidents, or the unintended consequences of unfortunate circumstances. Such deaths highlight the essential 'innocence' of the accused and the difficulty of establishing *mens rea*.

The primitive logic of such happenings is characteristic of precisely the type of mental functioning which Freud attributed to the unconscious mind, and named 'primary process' because he supposed it to be ontogenetically earliest. It implies a situation where in infancy (and in adult dream-states and mental disorders) thinking was held to be unchecked by the constraints of reality but followed instead the 'pleasure principle' so that '... whatever was thought of (wished for) was simply presented in a hallucinatory manner ...' (Freud 1912a, p. 219).

It was only, Freud hypothesised,[3] the non-occurrence of the expected satisfaction – the disappointment experienced – that led to the abandonment of this attempt at satisfaction by means of hallucination and to the generation of a more realistic perception of the external world.

In 'Mr Gilfil's Love-Story' (1858) Caterina is a young woman orphaned in infancy and spoiled by her adoptive parents, who treat her like a favourite toy but ignore her feelings. Captain Wybrow trifles with her affections, tells her that he loves her, and then submits to an arranged marriage with another woman. Caterina's love for him turns to hatred and scorn. On her way to a private meeting with him she impulsively conceals a dagger under her cloak:

'She has reached the Rookery, and is under the gloom of the interlacing boughs. Her heart throbs as if it would burst her bosom – as if every next leap must be its last. Wait, wait, O heart! – till she has done this one deed.

George Eliot's intense awareness of the destructive potential of female rage, and the murderous thoughts and acts of her heroines. A struggle with renunciation is necessary for them, she argues, because Eliot has internalised the patriarchal values of a corrupt Victorian social order.

3   Later psychoanalysts have elaborated this notion. Thus Melanie Klein saw frustration as an inevitable pain, generating the psychological defences of splitting and idealisation fundamental to the successful creation of an 'internal world', while Wilfred Bion suggested that it generated the function of 'thinking' in order to deal with the first 'thoughts' which the absent object called forth.

He will be there – he will be before her in a moment. He will come towards her with that false smile, thinking she does not know his baseness – she will plunge that dagger into his heart.

Poor child! poor child! She who used to cry to have the fish put back into the water – who never willingly killed the smallest living thing – dreams now, in the madness of her passion, that she can kill the man whose very voice unnerves her.

But what is that lying among the dark leaves on the path three yards before her?

Good God! it is he – lying motionless – his hat fallen off. He is ill, then – he has fainted. Her hand lets go the dagger, and she rushes towards him. His eyes are fixed, he does not see her. She sinks down on her knees, takes the dear head in her arms, and kisses the cold forehead. "Anthony, Anthony! speak to me – it is Tina – speak to me! O God, he is dead!"'

The coroner's verdict was that death had been imminent from long-established heart disease, though probably accelerated by some unusual emotion. Caterina, however, was driven nearly mad with guilt, and even the words of the loving Mr Gilfil were unable to reverse her enfeebled condition. They married: but she died shortly afterwards during pregnancy. The conflict in George Eliot's mind becomes evident when Mr Gilfil tries to console Caterina. He compares her to a baby bird who has no control over its emotions. 'You were like one of those little birds', he says. 'Your sorrow and suffering had taken such hold of you, you hardly knew what you did.' But Caterina responds to Mr Gilfil's comfort thus:

"'I don't know", she said, "I seemed to see him coming towards me, just as he would really have looked, and I meant – I meant to do it.'"

The central event in *Adam Bede* (1859), George Eliot's first novel, is infanticide. Hetty Sorrel murders her newborn baby by abandoning it in the woods. Our sympathy is, nevertheless, with her. She is the victim of Arthur, the young squire, with his complacent selfishness and irresponsibility in a casual relationship. Moreover, although convicted of murder and sentenced to hang, her confession to Dinah makes it clear that the crucial question of her intent to kill must be held in doubt.

"'I did do it. Dinah ... I buried it in the wood ... the little baby ... and it cried ... I heard it cry ... ever such a way off ... all night ... and I went back because it cried."

She paused, and then spoke hurriedly, in a louder, pleading tone. "But I thought perhaps it would not die – there might somebody find it. I did not kill it myself. I put it down there and covered it up, and when I came back it was gone."'

When Adam Bede, the hero, who is in love with Hetty, encounters Arthur earlier in the book, he too is involved in an episode where there is an equivocal death. He confronts Arthur with his self-indulgent behaviour and forces him to fight. In the heat of the fight Adam strikes a blow which seems to kill:

'But why did not Arthur rise? He was perfectly motionless, and the time seemed long to Adam ... Good God! had the blow been too much for him? Adam shuddered at the thought of his own strength, as with the oncoming of this dread he knelt down by Arthur's side and lifted his head from among the fern. There was no sign of life: the eyes and teeth were set. The horror that rushed over Adam completely mastered him and forced upon him its own belief. He could feel nothing but that death was in Arthur's face, and that he was helpless before it. He made not a single movement, but knelt like an image of despair gazing at an image of death.'

Arthur does not die, but it is clear that this is only determined by chance and that Adam is saved from sharing Hetty's fate through nothing but luck.[4]

Luck too comes to the rescue of Godfrey Cass, the eldest son of Squire Cass in *Silas Marner* (1861). Godfrey becomes entangled with a local prostitute and opium addict, Molly Farren, whom he makes pregnant. Although he is in love with Nancy Lammeter, he secretly marries Molly and then regrets having done so. He tells her that he would rather die than acknowledge her as his wife. Molly, on her way to a New Year's Eve party at the Squire's house where she plans to wreak vengeance by appearing in public with her child, gets lost in a snowstorm, takes opium to give herself courage, and apparently dies from hypothermia. When Godfrey hears of her death, George Eliot writes, he:

'... felt a great throb: there was one terror in his mind at that moment: it was, that the woman might *not* be dead. That was an evil terror – an ugly inmate to have found a nestling place in Godfrey's kindly disposition; but no disposition is a security from evil wishes to a man whose happiness hangs on duplicity.'

'The Lifted Veil', with its curious evocation of the supernatural, has been regarded by many as an aberration in George Eliot. Even her publisher, William Blackwood, thought it so at odds with her earlier work that he was reluctant to print it under her name. Nevertheless, the *leitmotif* of equivocal death, linking it unmistakably with her previous books, is clearly present.

After a serious illness, Latimer – the narrator of the story – falls passionately in love with his brother's fiancée Bertha. He grows to envy and hate his brother and rival in love. One day in a moment of weakness he confesses to Bertha his

---

4 Chance intervenes once more when his drunken father drowns at a time when Adam, full of anger, is certain he would 'live to be a thorn in his side'.

dream of marrying her. She is astonished and he immediately becomes ashamed of himself. The text continues:

'I wandered home slowly, entering our park through a private gate instead of the lodges. As I approached the house, I saw a man dashing off at full speed from the stable yard across the park. Had any accident happened at home? No; perhaps it was only one of my father's peremptory business errands that required this headlong haste. Nevertheless I quickened my pace without any distinct motive, and was soon at the house. I will not dwell on the scene I found there. My brother was dead – had been pitched from his horse, and killed on the spot by a concussion of the brain.'

A few pages earlier George Eliot had commented:

'Our tenderness and self-renunciation seem strong when our egoism has had its day – when, after our mean striving for a triumph that is to be another's loss, the triumph comes suddenly, and we shudder at it, because it is held out by the chill hand of death.'

The chill hand of death makes short shrift too of Mr Tulliver's moment of triumph over his lifelong enemy, lawyer Wakem, in *The Mill on the Floss* (1860). Tulliver had been the owner of Dorlcote Mill, but became bankrupt as a result of a series of ill-conceived legal suits against his neighbours, largely represented by Wakem. As a result, his son Tom's education had to be cut short, and Tulliver suffered a stroke on learning that the lawyer had taken over the mortgage on his Mill. Furthermore, on recovering he had no option but to continue to work there as a hired manager.

An opportunity for revenge presents itself when he encounters Wakem on horseback and manages to knock him off his mount. In a fit of rage Tulliver flogs him with his riding whip and releases his long pent-up hatred. But nemesis for this impulsive attack soon follows; Mr Tulliver takes to his bed and dies on the following day.

The heroine of *Romola* (1863) has been educated to assist her father in his classical researches. Like Dorothea in *Middlemarch*, she seems to be sacrificing herself, shut away from the world and devoted to an old, bookish man. Tito Melema becomes her father's secretary and she falls in love and marries him, dreaming of a 'triple life' in which the two of them will live in harmony, serving her father. But Tito rebels against this vision, spending less and less time at home, while the old blind scholar becomes progressively more depressed. Romola is caught between the two of them, unable to reconcile her loyalties.

At this point her father suddenly dies while she is in the process of taking dictation from him; and even with the first outburst of her sorrow, we are told, the irrepressible thought, 'Perhaps my life with Tito will be more perfect now', occurs.

'But the sense of something like guilt towards her father in a hope that grew out of his death, gave all the more force to the anxiety with which she dwelt on the means of fulfilling his supreme wish. That piety towards his memory was all the atonement she could make now for a thought that seemed akin to joy at his loss.'

In *Felix Holt* (1866) Mrs Transome, who like Gwendolen in *Daniel Deronda* was a beautiful, spoiled, and imperious girl, married a weak man whom she thought she could control. She had one son by him, Duffey, who turned out to be stupid, sickly and depraved. Then, after a brief and passionate affair with the young lawyer Jermyn, she had a second son, Harold, on whom she doted. However:

'The mother's early raptures had lasted but a short time, and even while that lasted there had grown up in the midst of them a hungry desire, like a black poisonous plant feeding in the sunlight – the desire that her first, rickety, ugly, imbecile child should die, and leave room for her darling, of whom she could be proud.'

Mrs Transome goes through life wishing Duffey dead, and eventually to her great joy he does die, leaving Harold, who is abroad and has become wealthy, heir to the estate. At last, she thinks, her darling son will return home and manage things in the way she desires. In fact he comes back a widower with a three-year-old child, and shows no affection towards his mother: nor does he allow her any say in the running of the property. He adds insult to injury by showing no interest in her Tory friends and even stands for Parliament as a Radical.

The consequences of any good fortune arising from another's death, in George Eliot's writing, are always fraught with danger and threaten the beneficiary. This is underlined by Lady Debarry, Mrs Transome's ill-natured 'friend', in an apparently casual aside, soon after she hears that the rich heir of the Transomes has actually returned home:

'These sudden turns of fortune are often dangerous to an excitable constitution … Poor Lady Alicia Methurst got heart disease from a sudden piece of luck – the death of her uncle, you know. If Mrs Transome were wise she would go to town – she can afford it now – and consult Dr Truncheon. I should say myself he would order her digitalis.'

George Eliot managed to weave no less than three equivocal deaths into the pattern of *Middlemarch*. First there is the case of Madame Laure, a Parisian actress with whom Lydgate, a young student of medicine at the time, falls in love. In a melodramatic performance she is required to stab her lover (played in reality by her husband), mistaking him for an evil duke. At the moment when the heroine is to enact the stabbing and her lover is to fall gracefully, we are told, '… the wife veritably stabbed her husband, who fell as death willed'. No motive is discovered for murder and after a legal investigation it is concluded that an accidental slip of the foot must have occurred; Madame Laure is released. Lydgate subsequently proposes marriage to her and while he is down on bended knee the following conversation occurs:

> "'I will tell you something", she said, in her cooing way, keeping her arms folded. "My foot really slipped.". "I know, I know", said Lydgate, deprecatingly. "It was a fatal accident – a dreadful stroke of calamity that bound me to you the more." Again Laure paused a little and then said, slowly, "*I meant to do it*."'

The second episode is the death of Mr Casaubon, the foolish and pedantic clergyman whom Dorothea Brooke marries in the mistaken belief that he is a great philosopher whose genius she will nurse while he works on an important project – a 'Key to All Mythologies'.

He soon turns against her. He despises her scholarly abilities, is totally selfish and inconsiderate, and becomes jealous of her growing friendship with his young cousin, Will Ladislaw. Dorothea is desperately unhappy; trapped in a catastrophic marriage, she has every reason to wish Casaubon dead.

At this point Mr Casaubon has his first heart attack, and Lydgate, his medical attendant, advises her that he could live for fifteen years or more, provided he is protected from mental agitation of all kinds. Casaubon wants to ensure that in the case of his death, Dorothea will devote herself to continuing his work, but she refuses to commit herself immediately and insists on having time to think about it overnight. Casaubon's tyrannical will is thwarted by her failure instantly to agree, and this infuriates him. The following day he dies, seemingly setting Dorothea free. But retribution of course comes swiftly; it is soon discovered that he has added a cruel codicil to his will, disqualifying her from inheriting the property if she marries Ladislaw.

The dénouement of the book involves the death of Raffles, a drunken rogue who is blackmailing Mr Bulstrode, to whom Lydgate has become indebted. Raffles, suffering from *delirium tremens*, is being cared for in Bulstrode's house, and Lydgate is called in for medical advice. He advises against the prevalent practice of continuing to allow alcohol and administering large does of opium. Instead, he gives detailed instructions to Bulstrode concerning the prescription of moderate doses of opium, emphasising the time at which they should cease, and forbidding all alcohol.

But Mr Bulstrode, who is struggling inwardly with his wish to kill Raffles, does not follow Lydgate's instructions. He forgets to tell Mrs Abel, his house-keeper, about limiting the dose of opium, and when Raffles's condition worsens, after a moment's hesitation, he gives her the key to his wine-cooler, where she can find brandy. Left to the care of Mrs Abel, Raffles dies during the night; and Mr Bulstrode, the following morning, finds an almost empty phial of opium and a used brandy bottle, which he proceeds to hide.

Bulstrode is culpable, for he both wished Raffles to die and failed to carry out medical instructions. Nevertheless there is an element of ambiguity, since he did not actually administer the fatal doses of opium or alcohol. Furthermore, Mrs Abel did no more than carry out what was widely accepted medical practice. An inquest concludes that death has occurred from natural causes; but nobody really believes it: Bulstrode remains under suspicion; and although Lydgate is officially vindicated all confidence in him is undermined, forcing him to give up his practice and leave Middlemarch.

Daniel Deronda was George Eliot's last novel, published when she was 57 years old; yet the equivocal death motif is as strong in it as in her first essays in fiction, eighteen years earlier. Gwendolen, a spoiled arrogant girl, suffers a setback when a financial disaster befalls her family. She marries the rich, languid and cruel Grandcourt, thinking that she can make use of him. Instead he bends her to his will, and within seven short weeks of marriage, we are told, her belief in her own power of dominating is utterly gone, and she is miserable. She grows to hate her husband. Then, during the course of a sailing trip he is apparently knocked overboard while putting about, and he drowns. Witnesses report that they heard a man cry out, and then heard a lady shriek and saw her throw herself into the water after him. This of course was Gwendolen, although it is uncertain whether she was intending to rescue Grandcourt or to commit suicide.

Later she confesses to Deronda that she had long wished her husband dead, and had even locked away a knife with which she meant to kill him (although she had subsequently thrown away the key). When he was knocked overboard by a gust of wind, he had risen above the surface several times, calling to her for a rope. She had frozen for a moment, holding on to the rope, but had not thrown it to him. George Eliot continues:

> 'Gwendolen's confession, for the very reason that her conscience made her dwell on the determining power of her evil thoughts, convinced him the more that there had been throughout a counterbalancing struggle of her better will. It seemed almost certain that her murderous thought had no outward effect – that, quite apart from it, the death was inevitable. Still, a question as to the outward effectiveness of a criminal desire dominant enough to impel even a momentary act, cannot alter our judgment of the desire; and Deronda shrank from putting that question forward in the first instance. He held it likely that Gwendolen's remorse aggravated her inward guilt, and that she gave the character of decisive action to what had been an unappreciably instantaneous glance of desire.'

When Johnny Cross (1884) wrote of George Eliot's childhood, he painted an idyllic picture which could not possibly have been true.

'The boy was his mother's pet and the girl her father's. They had everything to make children happy at Griff – a delightful old-fashioned garden – a pond, and the canal to fish in – and the farm offices close to the house – "the long cow-shed where generations of the milky mothers have stood patiently – the broad-shouldered barns where the old-fashioned flail once made resonant music", and where butter-making and cheese-making were carried on with great vigour by Mrs Evans.' (p.9)

Again, he described George Eliot's mother as:

'... a woman with an unusual amount of natural force – a shrewd practical person, with a considerable dash of the Mrs Poyser vein in her. Hers was an affectionate, warm-hearted nature, and her children on whom she cast "the benediction of her gaze" were thoroughly attached to her.' (p.7)

But George Eliot as a small child could not have experienced her mother as a strong and forceful person, for as Leslie Stephen (1902) informs us:

'Soon after her birth, her mother's health became weak;[5] the elder girl, Christiana, was sent to school; and Mary Anne with her brother spent part of every day at a dame-school close to their own gates.' (p.9)

The family had moved house when she was four or five months old, and her mother was responsible for two step-children (who left home shortly after the move), as well as Christiana and Isaac, George Eliot's older sister and brother. When she was five years old, Isaac too was sent away to school, and '... as her mother was still in bad health, she was sent to join her sister at school'. For the next three or four years she boarded at Miss Latham's in Attelborough, where she suffered from dreadful homesickness and night terrors, returning to Griff only on occasional Saturdays.

It is clear therefore that, far from being idyllic, George Eliot's early years must have been characterised by emotional insecurity and a series of disappointments, and separations from loved ones. Her brother Isaac, on whom Johnny Cross relied for information about her childhood, may have idealised this time, but the narrator in her short story 'The Lifted Veil' probably gives a more truthful picture when he says, 'My childhood perhaps seems happier to me than it really was', and, talking of his relationship with his mother:

'That unequalled love soon vanished out of my life, and even to my childish consciousness it was as if that life had become more still.'

---

5   According to the Hansons (1952), George Eliot's birth was actually the cause of her mother's ill-health.

George Eliot often indicated in later years that her childhood had been unhappy. For instance, in May 1844 she wrote to Sara Hennell:

'Childhood is only the beautiful and happy time in contemplation and retrospect: to the child it is full of deep sorrows, the meaning of which is unknown.'

All her biographers agree that George Eliot's mother became ill shortly after the birth of her last child, and it would appear that from then onwards, although she lived until 1836, her health was consistently poor. George Eliot was withdrawn from school at the age of sixteen in order to help nurse her mother during the last year of her life.

Little emphasis, however, has been placed on the reasons for Mrs Evans' ill-health or the circumstances surrounding its origin. Gordon Haight (1968)[6] mentions almost casually an important event not alluded to by previous biographers. On 16 March 1821. Mrs Evans gave birth to twin sons, named William and Thomas after her brothers. The twins lived for only ten days, and Haight tells us, 'Since the twins died Mrs Evans had not been well.' It is more than likely that her physical problems were compounded by a post-natal grief reaction. She probably became depressed, and as a result emotionally unavailable to her little girl, who was forced to develop psychological strategies for coping with the loss of her warm-hearted mother.

Mary Ann was just seven months old when her mother became pregnant with the twins. The birth of these two male siblings must have been a momentous event in her young life, and their tragic death just ten days later, when she was sixteen months old, must have left her with a psychological task of overwhelming proportions. If I am right in assuming that a seven-month-old child is old enough to appreciate in some sense that her mother is pregnant, then a seventeen-month-old child is certainly not too young to experience a complex mixture of feelings surrounding the birth and precipitate death of her younger brothers. If, as a seventeen-month-old baby, George Eliot wished that her newly-born twin brothers would disappear, her belief in the efficacy of wishful thinking would have been mightily confirmed, for they did indeed die just ten days after birth. This early confirmation of her destructive potential would make sense of her later repeated portrayal in fiction of situations where the external world, far from refuting unconscious phantasies, actually emphasises their omnipotent power.

---

6   Jennifer Uglow in her *George Eliot* (1987), also draws attention to the 'strange silence' on the subject of George Eliot's mother in biographies. She suggests: 'Perhaps the lack of response from her mother made her turn more positively to the energetic, exploring, managing world of her father and Isaac.'

The weight of parental experience and psychoanalytic inference supports the likelihood that feelings of hostility and rivalry towards new siblings are almost ubiquitous in small infants. Recent systematic research has also confirmed the complexity of ambivalent feelings in infants when a new baby is born. Deliberate naughtiness and aggressive acts towards the mother increased by a factor of three, and were particularly prone to occur during the period immediately following the birth (Dunne and Kendrick 1982).

Moreover, children aged around twelve months showed clear signs of a reparative urge, and were sensitive to others, frequently trying to comfort them when in distress. Their play in phantasy often revealed these interwoven and contrasting strands, and their behaviour showed a mixture of more 'grown up' independent activity as well as 'babyish' regressive clinging.

Whatever the exact nature of Mrs Evans's illness, and whenever the exact date of its onset, we can reasonably assume that it rendered her less able to respond sensitively to her infant daughter's needs. Joyce Robinson (1965) has reported lasting effects and damage to the development and relationships of two infants following the withdrawal of their mother's sensitive handling for just a fortnight, while Carr and Leared (1973) have described some of the consequences for a child of a more prolonged depression in his mother.

In this case the little boy was eighteen months old when his younger sister was born, and had two older sisters. The mother, although physically present, was felt to be emotionally unavailable by the child. He showed signs of precocious physical development, and was said by his mother 'never to have been a baby' – indeed, when shown a photograph of him standing in his playpen one author thought he looked '… in some strange way … more like a little old man than a baby.' He was so jealous of his sisters that his mother had to make elaborate plans to separate them, sending the older children to nursery school in the mornings, and having his baby sister cared for by the *au pair*. At night he was harnessed into his cot in order to prevent him from attacking his sisters, who slept in the same room.

Like the little boy whom Carr and Leared describe, George Eliot had an air of precocious adulthood about her from an early age. She was even called 'Little Mamma' by the older girls at Miss Latham's school.[7]

It would hardly be surprising if the infant Mary Ann had nursed hostile wishes toward her twin brothers. The fact that they died shortly after birth would only have served to confirm the child in a belief that her destructive wishes had omnipotent power, and were in every way equivalent to actions; whereas her

---

7   For a report of a seven-year follow-up linking precocious development of an infant girl with early deprivation resulting from maternal bereavement, see Martin James (1960). He observes that 'Her ideas ran away with her and if she thought a thing she was liable to act as though (by magic) it had already happened'. (pp.258–294)

reparative urges were weak and impotent. Her mother's prolonged sickness and withdrawal, beginning at this time, would indeed have seemed like swift retribution. If her own birth had been the original cause of her mother's ill-health, as the Hansons suggest, how much greater the sense of guilt regarding her destructiveness.

It is tempting to think that the roots of the self-doubt which plagued George Eliot,[8] and was so resistant to praise from friends or worldly success, are to be found in her early childhood. Certainly the opening lines on the title page of *Daniel Deronda* bear eloquent testimony to her lifelong concern with this problem:

> Let thy chief terror be of thine own soul:
> There, 'mid the throng of hurrying desires
> That trample o'er the dead to seize their spoil,
> Lurks vengeance, footless, irresistible
> As exhalations laden with slow death,
> And o'er the fairest troop of captured joys
> Breathes pallid pestilence.

---

8   G. H. Lewes explains in a letter why he kept reviews from her: 'Unhappily the habitual tone of her mind is distrust of herself, and no sympathy, no praise can do more than lift her out of it for a day or two'. (Eliot 1954, vol. 5, p.288).

14

Prejudice in Poetry
On Eliot and Pound

'We make out of the quarrel with others, rhetoric, but of the quarrel with ourselves, poetry', wrote W. B. Yeats (1917) calling into question the distinction between the two modes of discourse. In *T. S. Eliot and Prejudice*, Christopher Ricks (1988) concludes that this distinction hangs on the issue of responsibility:

> 'Rhetoric, being entirely instrumental, asks no questions. This is not irresponsible of it, but is a consequence of its being a-responsible. Art, though, does not exempt from its "suspicious and interrogating eye" its own procedures; art has eyes not only in the back of its head but also into the back of its head. The evil to which rhetoric may be put is not conceived of by the artist as something external to himself.' (p.8)

Art notwithstanding, the drowned Phoenician sailor of *The Waste Land* has no eyes to see in his watery grave – only pearls; and his unfortunate Jewish *Doppelgänger's* bulging eyeballs are in the process of being eaten away by crabs.[1] Ricks judges the ugliest touch of anti-Semitism in Eliot's poetry to be the first stanza of 'Dirge' posthumously published with the manuscript of *The Waste Land* in 1971.

> Full fathom five your Bleistein lies
> Under the flatfish and the squids.
> Graves' Disease in a dead jew's eyes!
> Where the crabs have eat the lids.
> Lower than the wharf rats dive
>   Though he suffer a sea-change
>   Still expensive rich and strange...

---

1   The prototype for these eyeball-eating crustaceans is said to have been Tristan Corbière's 'Le Bossu Bitor', *Gens de Mer 1861–68*, a chronic arthritic, relates the story of a hunchback who, after having intercourse, is tossed in a bedspread by prostitutes. The hunchback subsequently drowns himself out of shame, his wretched body having 'known love': '*Un cadavre bossu, ballonné démasqué / Par les crabes. Et ça fut jeté sur le quai.*'

All the elements of unselfconscious, vicious, anti-Jewish race-prejudice are here displayed – the association with slimy tentacular invertebrates, the overt link with vermin, the covert rhyme-suggestion of 'Yids', the apprehensive and envious conjunction of alien mystery with wealth and riches, and most notably the insistence that these characteristics are ineradicable and resist even the transforming processes of death. It was the immutability of the Jewish stigma that marked off modern biological anti-Semitism from its medieval counterpart (where conversion through taking the creed offered a remedy) and provided a 'public-health' justification for Hitler's 'Final Solution'.

Ezra Pound jotted on the manuscript of 'Dirge' '??doubtful', and Eliot added 'man's' above 'jew's' in a transitional draft. Can we infer that Eliot's 'dead jew' almost acquired the full status of a man, only to be dehumanised once again in the final version? Was he at some stage conceived by the artist as 'internal to himself' only to be rapidly evacuated? And were his eyes eaten out in order to avoid being met, the better to blind Eliot's conscience to his own inhumanity? The 'drowned Phoenician Sailor', 'a dead jew', and 'a dead man' are all homologues of 'thy father' in Ariel's song, and this strongly suggested to William Empson (Ricks 1988, p.46) where to look in Eliot's world for the object stimulating his hatred.

In 1940 Eliot had written: 'The Jewish religion is unfortunately not a very portable one, and shorn of its traditional practices, observances and Messianism, it tends to become a mild and colourless form of Unitarianism' (Ricks 1988, p.41) Christopher Ricks comments:

> 'The intersection of the Jewish and the Unitarian in this letter of Eliot's corroborates William Empson's inspired interpretation of the anti-Semitic impulses in the Waste Land manuscript (which harbours "Dirge") as intimate with Eliot's repudiation of his father and of his father's religion.' (p.44)

Such an analysis is entirely consistent with the kind of self-scrutiny that Eliot aspired toward, and which is so difficult to reconcile with his bigotry. Thus in 1935 Eliot wrote:

> 'The Church offers today the last asylum for one type of mind which the Middle Ages would hardly have expected to find among the faithful: that of the sceptic. Obviously I mean by sceptic, the man who suspects the origins of his own beliefs, as well as those of others; who is most suspicious of those which are passionately held: who is still more relentless towards his own beliefs than toward those of others; who suspects other people's motives because he has learned the deceitfulness of his own...' (p.9)

Yet one year later, he permitted an unsigned review to appear in *The Criterion* (1936):

> 'More particularly, it is noticeable that the jacket of the book speaks of the "extermination" of the Jews in Germany, whereas the title-page refers only to their "persecution", and as the title-page is to the jacket, so are the contents to the title-page, especially in the chapter devoted to the ill-treatment of Jews in German concentration camps.' (p.759–60)

We do make poetry out of the quarrel with ourselves, but we also make other things: neuroses, psychoses, addictions, perversions, religion, and prejudice. Eliot's prejudice was no inconsequential epiphenomenon, floating in the ether of social convention, but something inherent in his life and work. 'Dirge' was never published, to Eliot's credit: 'Burbank with a Baedeker: Bleistein with a Cigar' (1954) was, to his shame.

The difficulty for Eliot apologists in coming to terms with this, highlights the more general problem of prejudice with which Eliot was much preoccupied. Our perception of external reality is always coloured by preconception and expectation, and it is the subtle interplay of these *a priori* conditions with external stimuli that determines the form of experience. When Pound, for example, in a tantrum of frustration (Fuller Torrey 1984), rants about Englishmen being 'vermin', 'spirochetes' and 'pimps' with 'a talent for servility, sycophancy and bootlicking' (p.150) the mud does not stick. In the absence of a preconceived stereotype, his vitriol is neutralised, reduced to the absurd.

In aesthetics the problem revolves around our need to conjoin the 'beautiful' with the 'good'. If the juxtaposition of 'badness' with pleasing form always resulted in kitsch (Friedländer 1984) there would be no difficulty, we could invariably reject the art-work in question; but this is not the case. Our aesthetic response is disturbed precisely when we find unacceptable content embodied in compelling beauty – our preconceptions are violated.

> 'It is better not only as ultimately more complimentary to the best in Eliot but also as more illuminating of the poems and the depth of their life, to acknowledge that in so far as Eliot's poems are tinged with anti-Semitism, this – though lamentable – is not easily or neatly to be severed from things for which the poetry is not to be deplored or forgiven but actively praised.' (Ricks 1988, p.72)

If Eliot's mind was tinged with anti-Semitism, Ezra Pound's was engulfed by it, thus magnifying the quandary for appreciation of his poetry. It is this dilemma that provides the impetus for Robert Casillo's *The Genealogy of Demons* (1988). Having come to Pound's graveside in Venice, in order to pay homage and acknowledge his educational debt, Casillo was struck by the unholy contradiction:

> 'In spite of my admiration for Pound as a cultural figure, I had not forgotten his association with some of the most brutal and dehumanising ideologies of this century and the inseparable relation between these ideologies and his major poem. Nor could I forget that Pound, for all his love of Italy and desire for its "resurrection", as he called it, had served a regime which brought the country to degradation.' (p.vii)

The Genealogy of Demons links the personal development of Pound's anti-Semitism with the ideological ground that made it possible. In contrast to Christian anti-Semitism, rooted in the Middle Ages, which hinged on accusations of deicide and blood-libel, Voltaire — the 'patron saint' of modern anti-Semites — saw classical paganism as the authentic basis for Western European culture. Since Judaism was implacably opposed to pagan values, it was inherently alien to the West and thus unredeemable. It belonged to 'the Orient' and as such was hopelessly backward, 'historically arrested' and primitively attached to 'code-worship'. Nevertheless, Judaism was also (according to the German ethnologist and explorer Leo Frobenius) identified with modern Western rationalism, commercialism, and liberal civilisation as opposed to the simple agrarian-based culture of pre-industrial times. The Jews were therefore responsible for having torn men away from the earth.

Pound embraced all these ideas, and in addition gave credence to the notion of a 'Jewish Conspiracy' for world domination, as adumbrated in *The Protocols of the Elders of Zion* — that infamous turn-of-the-century Russian forgery, promoted and distributed widely in the 1920s by Nazi sympathisers (Cohn 1967). In fact, as Casillo demonstrates, these ideas came to dominate Pound's work and form 'the deep structure of the Poundian worldview'.

What emerges is a picture of deep-seated intellectual and emotional confusion, where Fascism is seen as a life-affirming force, creating order and clarity, while 'the Jews' are the epitome of destructiveness, promoting conflict and ultimately representing the disintegration of all values into an undifferentiated miasma. Pound's reaction to the character of Leopold Bloom in *Ulysses* spells this out quite clearly: 'Ulysses is a summary of pre-war Europe', he wrote in 1933, 'the blackness and mess and muddle of a "civilisation" led by disguised forces and a bought press the general sloppiness, the plight of the individual intelligence in that mess! Bloom very much *is* the mess' (quoted in Carpenter 1988, p.319).

'The swamp', we are reminded, had a profound significance for the fascist mind, and there are many examples in Pound's writing where he invokes this imagery.[2] Thus in 1942 he speaks of the Jews as a 'poison' which 'already by the

---

2 Is it too far-fetched to note here that Pound's paternal grand-mother, Sarah, was a descendant of

time of Scotus Erigena ... had begun to make a bog of things'. The same Jews are also held responsible for all the oppressive restrictions imposed upon behaviour by Christian ethics! 'Throughout Pound's writings, Casillo (1988) shows us:

> '...as throughout Enlightenment and Orientalist anti-Semitism, one encounters a sinister, contradictory, and finally paradoxical image of the Jews. Like the Near East, they combine but never reconcile the qualities of Nature and anti-Nature, passivity and aggressiveness, fertility and sterility, abstraction and materialism, the patriarchal and matriarchal, the masculine (Jehovah) and the feminine (Cybele), the anti-natural and the anti-historical, the desert and the swamp.' (p.84)

The range of loathsome and contradictory qualities which Pound managed to press 'the Jews' into representing is indeed extraordinary – the only consistent characteristic appearing to be their troublesome nature as incubi that he himself needed to expel. They testify, as Casillo says, 'not to any confusion in the Jewish "object"', but rather to the uncertain elements of Pound's own identity.

It is, for example, a fine irony to hear Pound in Canto 35 (1965) railing against Jewish cowardice, as represented by 'Mr Corles' who, as a 'commander of machine guns' left his post but escaped court martial by having his family send him to a 'mind sanatorium'. In reality, it was Pound who in 1945 escaped trial for treason by being declared insane and unfit to plead. he was subsequently confined for thirteen years in St Elizabeth Hospital, where he continued to express fascist and anti-Semitic beliefs. On arriving in Italy after his release, he gave the Fascist salute to reporters and complained to friends about the 'Jew Pork Herald Tribune'.

By 1942 T. S. Eliot, then 54 years of age, had mellowed. His antipathy toward 'free-thinking Jews', if still present, was no longer expressed. The tone of his poetry was no longer hectoring and superior, the innuendo of names (Rachel née Rabinovitch, Bleistein, etc.) had disappeared; the anti-Semitism of his earlier work had apparently gone. In its place came a sense of reflective acceptance, acknowledgement of wrongdoing, and a regret most poignantly rendered in his poem 'Little Gidding' in the last of the 'gifts reserved for age'.

> And last, the rending pain of re-enactment
> > Of all that you have done, and been; the shame
> > Of motives late revealed, and the awareness
> Of things ill done and done to others' harm
> > Which once you took for exercise of virtue.

---

the esteemed New England Loomis family? Pound was proud of his ancestry, but learnt while at college that his branch of the family was 'rotten' – in fact Sarah's grandfather was a horse-thief and murderer, who led the Loomis Gang, notorious for terrorising the surrounding countryside from their ranch at Nine Mile Swamp, in upstate New York.

At the same time as Eliot wrote this, Pound's wartime propaganda broadcasts from Italy were in full flood, pouring out vituperative racist libel two or three times a week, blaming the Jews for both World Wars and for all else that was wrong with the world. Thus, on 9 April 1942:

> 'I think Roosevelt belongs in an insane asylum now. His writers are lunatics. You have come down far when a Jew by the name of Finkelstein runs your country. ... I don't want the United States to use Hawaii in the interest of a kike ... the United States has been invaded by vermin ...' (Fuller Torrey 1984, pp.264, 162)

Pound's insight was longer in coming, and when it did, lacked the gentleness of Eliot's resignation. Canto 116 (1966), written in his seventy-fifth year, is a harrowing and beautiful record of the struggle:

> I have brought the great ball of Crystal; who can lift it?
> Can you enter the great acorn of light?
> But the beauty is not the madness
> Tho' my errors and wrecks lie about me.
> And I am not a demigod,
> I cannot make it cohere
> If love be not in the house there is nothing.
> The voice of famine unheard.
> How came beauty against this blackness ...
>
> To confess wrong without losing rightness:
> Charity I have had sometimes,
> I cannot make it flow thru.
> A little light, like a rushlight to lead back to splendour.

Here indeed we can see poetry, not propaganda, being made out of Pound's inner struggle. Perhaps his best work? But the cost would appear to have been high, for his last years were bedeviled by intractable melancholia, the struggle to take responsibility for his 'wrecks' apparently lost. In 1967, Allen Ginsberg, the American, Jewish, Buddhist poet, visited him in Venice, bringing marijuana and Beatles records. In a surrealist scene, he coaxed the mono-syllabic and depressed octogenarian into a conversation; whereupon Pound, having spent a lifetime inciting others into hatred of the Jews, and more than two decades after the Holocaust, uttered one often-quoted line repudiating anti-Semitism —'But the worst mistake I made was that stupid, suburban prejudice ...' (Carpenter 1988, p.899).

Does any of this matter, now that prejudice is no longer chic in literary circles? Now that we are all 'Jews', all uprooted (and not like the camps of the early modernists, 'full of facists, fascist sympathisers and other lovers of on-time trains'), it is alleged to be fact that in contemporary society what writers say matters not a whit (see Graham 1988, Gass 1989).

This may have seemed comfortably and frustratingly true for liberal democracies, often thought of as somehow isolated from other political systems, but in the wake of the Salman Rushdie affair, the immense potential significance of what writers say must surely be acknowledged. It would appear, then, that we are not yet all 'Jews', content to accommodate ourselves to the diaspora of uncertainty. Far from it. In the modern world, the resurgence of religious fundamentalism offers an anodyne to precisely the same human dilemmas that previously produced fascism.

And does it matter for art, now that we are all post-modernists in poetry, taking for granted the Poundian revolution? Poets need to discern the nature of the interior material made available to them, and to know what they are doing with it. Anti-Semitism makes poetry bad, because it is predicated on a flight from internal reality. It gives expression not to a true conflict but to a false solution. It offers itself as 'the King of Myths', the ultimate cliché – infinitely plastic, infinitely malleable 'the Jews' are capable of being made to symbolise anything, and imaginative work is thereby pre-empted. Mindless prejudice is, without doubt, the enemy of poetry.

15
Dark Corners
On Poetry and Melancholy

Sylvia Plath's last poem is terrifyingly beautiful. Written just one week before she took her life, 'Edge' is a consummate work of art, and yet it is all wrong (if a poem can be wrong).[1] The heart cries out against it – auguring, as it does, the death of the poet, not only in art but in reality. Some dreadful confusion has clearly taken place.

> The woman is perfected.
> Her dead
>
> Body wears the smile of accomplishment,
> The illusion of a Greek necessity
>
> Flows in the scrolls of her toga,
> Her bare
>
> Feet seem to be saying:
> We have come so far, it is over.
>
> Each dead child coiled, a white serpent,
> One at each little   .
>
> Pitcher of milk, now empty,
> She has folded
>
> Them back into her body as petals
> Of a rose close when the garden
>
> Stiffens and odors bleed
> From the sweet, deep throats of the night flower.
>
> The moon has nothing to be sad about,
> Staring from her hood of bone.
>
> She is used to this sort of thing.
> Her blacks crackle and drag. ('Edge' Plath 1981)

---

1   'Edge' from *Ariel* is quoted by permission of Faber and Faber Limited and Harper Collins Publishers.

The empty pitchers of milk, redolent of Plath's own dried-up breasts, were transformed on the night of her suicide into full cups of milk which she left out for the children; the scrolls of the toga became towels and cloths, mercifully stuffed under their bedroom door to save them from the gas. A devastating, twisted logic – as David Holbrook (1988) demonstrates – allowed her to act:

> 'She was anxious that her children should have their drinks next morning.
> A parallel anxiety did not stop her from orphaning them.' (p.277)

Would that the tragic 'necessity' for her own death had remained an illusion.

If Sylvia Plath were alive today, she would be a much older woman, continuing no doubt to enrich our lives with her work. Instead, her sadly abbreviated life is somehow fixed in our minds, infinitely rehearsing and repeating the suicidal act. However, when Philip Larkin (1983) suggested that the value of her work depends on '... how highly we rank the expression of experience with which we can in no sense identify, and from which we can only turn in shock and sorrow' (p.281), he was surely mistaken, seeking perhaps to distance himself and the reader from the full horror of its implications.

Far from being strangely removed from everyday experience, Plath's work accurately evokes a universal caesura in the human condition. It is for this reason that her posthumous fame has never ceased to grow, generating numerous studies and at least two major biographical attempts. In the second of these, *Bitter Fame*, Anne Stevenson (1989a) writes:

> '...many people, especially women, discovered in her work a shocking revelation of extremist elements in their own psyches. Plath became a spokeswoman for the angry, the disillusioned, the bewildered generations of the 1960s and 1970s. The tragedy of her suicide and the power of her last poems seemed to sweep the polarities of life and art (carefully separated by T.S. Eliot and the New Critics) into one unanswerably dramatic gesture of female defiance: "The blood jet is poetry, / There is no stopping it".' (p.xi)

In the years after her death a feminist myth took shape which portrayed Sylvia Plath, not as the victim of a lost inner struggle, but as a sacrifice on the altar of masculine narcissism (her gravestone, bearing her married name, has been desecrated by vandals). It is part of Anne Stevenson's purpose, with the blessing of the Plath Estate, to explode the myth and replace it with an objective account. But such explosions, though planned, are always in danger of becoming uncontrolled.

Linda Wagner-Martin's *Sylvia Plath: A Biography* (1988a)[2] erred in failing to confront this myth, but at least it avoided the oversimplified and contradictory reductivism of Anne Stevenson's supposed insights. In *Bitter Fame* we are told, for instance, that the unseen menace that haunts nearly everything that Plath wrote is attributable to her having undergone electro-convulsive therapy in 1959; and conversely that her lack of progress following admission to McLean Hospital was halted by a short course of ECT, to which she had a positive reaction. Stevenson forgets that Plath was taking sleeping pills routinely at the age of fourteen, and that her suicidal impulses antedated her contact with the psychiatrists. Indeed, it was an episode of self-mutilation that precipitated the original referral. Above all, Anne Stevenson overlooks the 'menace' so obviously present in the 'Juvenilia', all written before 1956. One example will suffice:

> Like a diver on a lofty spar of land
> Atop the flight of stairs I stand.
> A whirlpool leers at me,
> Absorbent sponge;
> I cast off my identity
> And make the fatal plunge. ('Family Reunion', Plath 1981)

Something unseemly has crept into *Bitter Fame* – almost, one senses, against its author's better judgment. As A. Alvarez (1989) has commented:

> 'In more than 350 pages of disparagement, nothing is said of Plath's charm, which was considerable, or of her quizzical intelligence and profound love of poetry, or of her courage and resilience in her last ghastly months.' (pp.34–36)

In an effort to score 'objective' psychological points and expose the 'underlying true self' of her subject, Stevenson is carried away by the injurious accounts of a few informants, and seems to achieve merely an extraordinary lack of compassion. During her first attempt at love-making, Sylvia Plath, according to a friend, was unfortunate enough to sustain a vaginal tear which continued to haemorrhage on the following day. Anne Stevenson's (1989a) description continues:

> 'Though shaken herself, Nancy was surprised by the force of Sylvia's terror. As she lay in a pool of blood on the bathroom floor, fear invaded the room "like a third person". When the mantle of self-possession fell apart, "all the stored-up fear and vulnerability came pouring out in a confusing helter-skelter of words and sobs".' (p.54)

To be sure, one needs no secret store of fear and vulnerability to be terrified in such circumstances, yet Anne Stevenson offers the account in evidence of Plath's underlying mental instability. Her tone here acquires a harsh and spurious 'objectivity' which ill becomes a biographer.

---

2   See also *Sylvia Plath: The Critical Heritage* (Wagner-Martin 1988b).

Of course, a poet may be uncomfortable with investigative work. Stevenson's own poem, 'Hot Wind, Hard Rain' (1989b) dedicated to Sylvia Plath, contains the following lines:

> Hot winds bring on hard rain, and here in Durham
> a downpour tonight will probably allay
> Whatever has got the willows by the hair,
> Shoving light under their leaves
>   like an indecent surgeon.

This is not to say that 'the all-American-girl' revealed by Plath's mother in *Letters Home* (A.S. Plath 1976) and 'the precarious narcissist' of *Bitter Fame* never existed, rather that these were not polarities between false and true selves, but alternative states of mind in a complex kaleidoscope of identity. To confuse inner and outer worlds and mistake the part for the whole is to commit the same error that Plath fell into.

Anne Stevenson's (1989a) biggest mistake is to set Sylvia Plath's interior life in a seemingly unfamiliar and alien world. Plath's poetry, rather than casting light on psychological processes to which we are all in some degree vulnerable, is made to reflect only her inaccessible mental aberration. Whether or not 'Event' and 'The Rabbit Catcher' were set off by an upsurge of pathological jealousy, the poems give no grounds for concluding that:

> '[Sylvia Plath] was making her self-justifying and unforgiving case in much the same terms as henceforth she would use to sow "the seeds of the myth of her martyrdom" in presenting her situation to friends and to her mother. In this concept she herself appears guiltless; her children are used to substantiate her role. Her husband is demeaned and blamed...' (p.245)

On the contrary, the voice of 'Event' (Plath 1981) is non-judgmental, perplexed, descriptive. It brings together both partners in the grip of a force perceived as greater than themselves, bewildered by the power of un-love.

> Where apple bloom ices the night
> I walk in a ring,
> A groove of old faults, deep and bitter.
>
> Love cannot come here.
> A black gap discloses itself.
> On the opposite lip
>
> A small white soul is waving, a small white maggot.
> My limbs, also, have left me.
> Who has dismembered us?
>
> The dark is melting. We touch like cripples. ('Event', Plath 1981)

Precisely because Plath's poetry invariably attains this integrity, so accurately and unflinchingly charts the inner happenings, we are taken aback by her capacity for confusion in the outer world. She reverses the expected state of affairs. It is as if she could see clearly in one direction only — inwards – while apprehending the outer world through some distorting opacity.

Is this the tribute that poetry exacts? Perhaps confusion between internal and external reality and vulnerability to melancholia is an occupational hazard for poets. Certainly Jeremy Reed (1989) sees poetic activity as inherently dangerous:

> '... the risk involved in writing poetry is the risk of the migrant bird on a stormy night. Either we navigate a return journey around a focal beacon of inner space, or like the shearwater we stun ourselves against a lighthouse cupola, and must depend on the lighthouse man to throw us back into the air.' (p.137)

The poet in his exploration of inner space is forever in danger of finding himself unable to return. Reed's empathic study gathers together essays on a gallery of poets, ranging from John Clare and Christopher Smart to Robert Lowell, Theodore Roethke, and Hart Crane. Lush with tropes and conceits, the book is a poem in its own right. While Gerard Manley Hopkins's contemporaries '... nosed downstream into oblivion, he forced himself against the current. He was a salmon migrating upstream ...' Baudelaire was 'a man who lived in a mirror'; a Lowell poem '... stands out like the triangular dorsal fin of a shark cutting the surface of blue inshore waters' (p.35).

Hopkins was subject to melancholy all his life, but the year 1885, when he was lecturing on Classics at University College, Dublin, appears to have marked his lowest ebb. 'When I am at the worst', he wrote to Alexander Baillie, 'though my judgment is never affected, my state is much like madness' (Reed 1989, p.35) In this he was certainly correct, for no matter how deep his depression, Hopkins's grasp on reality never faltered. The predominant emotion in his poems is unquestionably awe; he is only too aware of the 'otherness' of the natural world. In contrast to Sylvia Plath, there is no hint of romantic fusion in his vision of death:

> O the mind, mind has mountains; cliffs of fall
> Frightful, sheer, no man fathomed. Hold them cheap
> May who ne'er hung there. Nor does long our small
> Durance deal with that steep or deep. Here! creep
> Wretch, under a comfort serves in a whirlwind: all
> Life death does end and each day dies with sleep. (Hopkins 1970)

Rainer Maria Rilke, too, endured periods of profound depression; and his suffering and fear of poetic sterility are expressed in strikingly similar tones (1967):

> Tears will not let me speak.
> My death, blackamoor, heart-keeper!
> tip me down deeper, steeper,
> pour them off. For I want to speak.
>
> Giant black heart-holder, would in the end,
> because I'd spoken,
> silence even then have been broken?
>
> Rock me, old friend!

The image of the inexpressible abyss, the spectre of falling into and being engulfed by emptiness haunts these poets. 'What if the voice never returns', says Jeremy Reed (1989) 'or falls short of work already completed? This is the poet's constant anxiety; he may become an empty vessel...'

Sylvia Plath seems to confront this kind of anxiety head-long. Perpetually tempted by the oceanic urge, she is ready to fling herself into emptiness like a free-fall parachutist:

> I didn't want any flowers, I only wanted
> To lie with my hands turned up and be utterly empty.
> How free it is, you have no idea how free – ('Tulips', Plath 1981)

Plath attended Robert Lowell's writing seminar at Boston University in 1959, and in an acerbic memoir appended to Anne Stevenson's biography Dido Merwin suggests that the two poets had more than a little in common: 'The pattern of their public scenes was remarkably similar except that he used words like a Tommy gun whereas she used silence like nerve gas' (p.336) Their private scenes, too, were not unalike: compare Plath's

> Now the room is ahiss. The instrument
> Withdraws its tentacle.
> But the spawn percolate in my heart...
>
> ('Words Heard by Accident, Over the Phone', Plath 1981)

with Lowell's

> I nursed my last clear breath of oxygen,
> there, waiting for the chandelier to fall,
> tentacles clawing for my jugular. ('The Severed Head' Reed 1989, p.101)

What function does poetry serve for the poet? Lowell came to question whether his method of composition was 'a death-rope or a lifeline'. Jeremy Reed sees it as unquestionably the latter, but in Plath's case the answer is not so clear. Although writing appeared to make her happy – transforming hurt and beauty into words, as she put it in her Summer 1950 journal (Wagner-Martin 1988a, p.55) – it may also have contributed to her death. For artistic expression, as A. Alvarez (1971) has pointed out, is not always therapeutic; the artist does not necessarily enjoy some kind of cathartic relief:

'Instead, by some perverse logic of creation, the act of formal expression may simply make the dredged-up material more readily available to him. The result of handling it in his work may well be that he finds himself living it out.' (p.32)

Jeremy Reed concludes that a poet's only biographer is his double: 'It is what happens in the dark corners, in the hours when one is unrestrainably alone, that comprises the record of one's life.' Sylvia Plath has left us a graphic account of those dark places.

16

Robert Louis Oedipus

'...half unconsciously, half in a wilful blindness, she continued to undermine her husband with his son. As long as Archie remained silent, she did so ruthlessly, with a single eye to heaven and the child's salvation; but the day came when Archie spoke. It was 1801, and Archie was seven, and beyond his years for curiosity and logic, when he brought the case up openly. If judging were sinful and forbidden, how came papa to be a judge? to have that sin for a trade? to bear the name of it for a distinction?

"I can't see it," said the little Rabbi, and wagged his head.

Mrs. Weir abounded in commonplace replies.

"No, I cannae see it," reiterated Archie. "And I'll tell you what, mamma, I don't think you and me's justified in staying with him."

The woman woke to remorse; she saw herself disloyal to her man, her sovereign and bread-winner, in whom (with what she had of worldliness) she took a certain subdued pride. She expatiated in reply on my lord's honour and greatness; his useful services in this world of sorrow and wrong, and the place in which he stood, far above where babes and innocents could hope to see or criticise. But she had builded too well – Archie had his answers pat: Were not babes and innocents the type of the kingdom of heaven? Were not honour and greatness the badges of the world? And at any rate, how about the mob that had once seethed about the carriage?

"It's all very fine," he concluded, "but in my opinion, papa has no right to be it. And it seems that's not the worst yet of it. It seems he's called 'the Hanging Judge" – it seems he's crooool. I'll tell you what it is, mamma, there's a tex' borne in upon me: It were better for that man if a milestone were bound upon his back and him flung into the deepest most pairts of the sea.' (Stevenson 1896, p.24–5)

I am glad of this opportunity to share my enthusiasm for Robert Louis Stevenson. To what extent this enthusiasm derives from a narcissistic identification with the author I will leave you to judge, but I feel it necessary to confess at the outset that my second name is Robert, my father's name was Louis, and I would be gladly known as Stephen Robert Louison!

Over and above the wit and elegance of his writing, I have been dazzled by the profundity of Stevenson's psychological insight and constantly taken aback by the extraordinarily modern relevance of his ideas. Yet Stevenson died in 1894, just about six months before the epoch making publication of Freud's *Studies on Hysteria*. So although their lives overlapped, and both men contributed to the Proceedings of the Society for Psychical Research (that curious reaction of late nineteenth century Cambridge to the materialism of its time, which dedicated itself to the scientific proof of life after death) (Pines 1990), Stevenson belongs firmly in the pre-psychoanalytic era.

John Carey (1993), writing in the *Sunday Times,* justly noted a snag for Stevenson biographers – he wrote his own life unmatchably in essays and stories, 'He worked at his style like a diamond cutter, and responded to sensations with the delicacy of a poetical geiger counter...'. The choice is therefore between simply quoting page after page, or substituting one's own dull words. I need not crave your indulgence, therefore, if I quote liberally during the course of this chapter.

Little Archie in *Weir of Hermiston*, made no attempt whatsoever to understand the man with whom he dined and breakfasted – for as Stevenson (1896) tells us in an aside that prefigures Freud's first principle of mental functioning, 'Parsimony of pain, glut of pleasure, these are the two alternating ends of youth; and Archie was parsimonious' (p.45). When the wind blew cold out of a certain quarter, he turned his back on it; stayed as little as was possible in his father's presence.

As we know, he eventually came publicly to denounce his father as a judicial murderer, and though he regretted it almost immediately, was obliged to discontinue his studies at the Bar and retire to the country as a kind of recluse, whereupon he encountered Kirstie, a family retainer old enough to be his mother who was instantly besotted with him. As luck would have it Kirstie had an eponymous niece of more appropriate age, Kirstie 2, with whom Archie duly fell in love.

Stevenson died in Samoa while he was writing the 'Weir', but his step-daughter and devoted amenuensis, Mrs Strong, was able to pass on the intended argument of the story. Frank Innes, a false friend seduces young Kirstie 2, and Archie then kills Frank, presumably a crime of passion. He is tried before his own father, found guilty and condemned to death, manages to escape from prison and ultimately reach America with his beloved Kirstie.

What of his father the Weir? The ordeal in taking part in the trial of his own son proves too much for the Lord Justice Clerk, and he dies of the shock.

'An absurd and unlikely tale', I hear an uncouth voice cry, 'and so what if a man in his dying days writes about a son who is a murderer and a father who drops dead after sentencing his son?'

Stevenson, called 'Louis' by his family, was born in 1850, the only child of Thomas a civil engineer from a family with a tradition of lighthouse building, and the youngest daughter, Margaret, of the Revd. Lewis Balfour. Tall, slender and graceful with bright grey eyes and smiling mouth, she has been described as in many ways the polar opposite of her husband. Where he was emotionally demonstrative, outspoken, dogmatic and given to violent swings of mood, she is said to have been cultivated, companionable, affectionate and a born optimist, with a noticeable talent for shutting her eyes to trouble or ignoring it rather than finding solutions.

I am reminded of Stevenson's (Balfour 1901) description of Mr Henry in *The Master of Ballantrae*:

'...His whole mind stood open to happy impressions, welcoming these and making much of them; but the smallest suggestion of trouble or sorrow he received with visible impatience, and dismissed again with immediate relief. It was to this temper that he owed the felicity of his later days; and yet here it was, if anywhere, that you could call the man insane. A great part of this life consists in contemplating what we cannot cure; but Mr. Henry, if he could not dismiss solicitude by an effort of the mind, must instantly and at whatever cost annihilate the cause of it; so that he played alternately the ostrich and the bull.' (p.134)

Here is Margaret Stevenson revealing her character when she tells the story of one of the only letters from Louis she failed to keep:

'In the spring of 1872 Louis was in a very depressed state; he wrote one terribly morbid letter to me from Dunblane, all about death and churchyards – it vexed me so much that I put it in the fire at once. Years after, when he was writing his essay *Old Mortality*, he applied to me for that letter, and was quite vexed when I told him that I had destroyed it.' (p.27)

But Stevenson's mother, though she outlived him, was a valetudinarian. Chronically sick, she is reputed to have never risen from her bed before noon during the first thirteen years of his life, and his father was often away for long periods on business. He may have acquired tuberculosis from his mother at the age of two. In any event she found herself unable to look after him and was forced, she said, to give him over almost entirely into the hands of hired nurses.

The first was discovered drunk in a pub while the baby Stevenson, wrapped up in a parcel was tucked away out of sight on a shelf behind a bar. There were two or three more failures before, at the age of eighteen months, a nurse called Alison Cunningham, with a strict Calvinist religion, took over his care and began a lifelong association.

The small boy would lie in bed racked by his cough and, as he later recalled, 'praying for sleep or morning from the bottom of my shaken little body', only to wake in terror from a feverish sleep, and be lifted out of bed into the hands of his watchful nurse Cummy. To what extent his night-terrors were actually a product of the hell-fire and brimstone with which she filled his mind, and his insomnia exacerbated by the coffee Cummy fed him to sooth away his pain, one can only speculate. Of Stevenson's own affection for her, there can be no doubt, tenderly expressed in his dedication to *A Child's Garden of Verses* (1885):

> 'For all the story-books you read;
> For all the pains you comforted:
> For all you pitied, all you bore,
> In sad and happy days of yore;
> My second Mother, my first Wife,
> The angel of my infant life.'

The easy apposition of the words mother and wife, deliberately capitalised by Stevenson in this poem, engages our attention and presages my theme.

Nick-named 'Smout' after the small-fry of the salmon, by his fond parents, Stevenson was an affectionate child and remained deeply attached to both of them throughout his life. But the contours of his underlying protective concern for mother and ambivalent conflict with father are hinted at in some of the earliest records of his childhood. At the age of three, for example, alone with his mother one day after dinner, and having seen his nurse cover her mistress with a shawl at such times, he took a doyley off the table, unfolded it, and carefully spread it over her saying 'That's a wee bittie, Mama'. Again, in 1854 his mother noted: 'Smout got a sword for his Christmas present. When his father was disparaging it he said 'I can tell you Papa, it's a silver sword and a gold sheath and the boy's well off and quite contented' (Balfour 1901, p.27)). He was less contented two weeks later, when made to wear a shawl that obscured his sword, for his mother noted that he became distressed that he would not look like a soldier.

One may wonder why pater Stevenson was disparaging his little son's Christmas present; however this may be, the boy's vision of soldierly independence was not to come about. Stevenson remained financially dependent upon his father throughout that gentleman's life, and naturally became more irked by his position as time went on.

When he was eleven his parents instituted a system of fines for any strong words he used, and in April 1866, still a dutiful sixteen-year-old, we find him writing playfully to his father:

'RESPECTED PATERNAL RELATIVE, – I write to make a request of the most moderate nature. Every year I have cost you an enormous – nay, elephantine – sum of money for drugs and physician's fees, and the most expensive time of the whole twelve months was March.

But this year the biting Oriental blasts, the howling tempests, and the general ailments of the human race have been successfully braved by yours truly.

Does not this deserve remuneration?

I appeal to your charity. I appeal to your generosity, I appeal to your justice, I appeal to your accounts, I appeal in fine, to your purse.

My sense of generosity forbids the receipt of more – my sense of justice forbids the receipt of less – than half-a-crown. – Greeting from Sir, your most affectionate and needy son.' (Colvin 1901, p.8)

Graham Balfour, Stevenson's first biographer, (1901) described the relationship between father and son as largely harmonious:

'The differences between the pair were slight, the points of resemblance many. The younger man devoted his life to art and not to science, and the hold of dogma upon him was early relaxed. But the humour and the melancholy, the sterness and the softness, the attachments and the prejudices, the chivalry, the generosity, the Celtic temperament, and the sensitive conscience passed direct from father to son in proportions but slightly varied, and to some who knew them both well the father was the more remarkable of the two. One period of misunderstanding they had, but it was brief, and might have been avoided had either of the pair been less sincere or less in earnest. Afterwards, and perhaps as a consequence, their comprehension and appreciation of each other grew complete, and their attachment was even deeper than that usually subsisting between father and only son...' (p.24)

But this version seems at best economical with the *actualité*, given the magnitude of feeling and the fact that the conflict manifestly endured for at least ten years, between 1870 and 1880, when Stevenson's father threatened to disinherit him.

Flora Masson (1922) captured the nascent rivalry coming to the surface in a graphic account of a dinner party, held in the Stevenson household:

'Our end of the table was, to me, almost uncomfortably brilliant. Mr Stevenson had taken me in, and Louis Stevenson was on my other side. Father and son both talked, taking diametrically opposed points of view on all things under the sun. Mr Stevenson seemed to me, on that evening, to be the type of the kindly Edinburgh father... But Louis Stevenson, on my other side, was on that evening in one of his most recklessly brilliant moods. His talk was almost incessant. I remember feeling quite dazed at the amount of intellection he expended on each subject, however trivial in itself, that he landed upon. He worried it as a dog might worry a rat, and he threw it off lightly, as some chance word or allusion set him thinking and talking of something else. The father's face at certain moments was a study – an indescribable mixture of vexation, fatherly pride and admiration, and sheer bewilderment at the boy's brilliant flippancies and quick thrust of his wit and criticism.' (p.127)

By 1873 Stevenson was in the midst of a full scale late adolescent war with his paternal relative, and though there was no obvious end to his continued dependence (given his chosen lifestyle) he was finding it unbearable – 'How miserable that is becoming to me', he writes to Mrs Frances Sitwell (Booth and Mehew 1994), 'I cannot endure to be dependent much longer. It stops my mouth.'

It seems likely that Stevenson contracted syphilis during his University years, thus adding a second infectious granuloma to his pre-existing tuberculosis. Known as 'Velvet Jacket', he appears to have been a favourite among the *filles de joie*, one of whom is said to have spent so much time in his company that she was eventually beaten up by the brothel keeper for neglect of duty. Early biographers concur in stating that it was extreme pressure from his parents, including a threat to disown him, that brought this relationship to an end.

But the ostensible cause of his split with father, was the discovery by Thomas on the last day of January 1873, of the constitution of the Liberty, Justice and Reverence Club, of which Stevenson and his cousin Bob were founder members. The club advocated socialism, atheism, abolition of the House of Lords and the disregard of everything taught to you by your parents. Stevenson had broken with Christianity.

In an impossible attempt to straighten out his son, Thomas sent him to stay in Suffolk with his cousin Maud Babbington, for a 'cooling off' period; where on arrival he met and became infatuated with Frances Sitwell. Mrs Sitwell was twelve years his senior, estranged from her husband and the mother of a small son; it was said of her that she had more men in love with her than any other woman then living, though Oscar Wilde (perhaps immune to her attractions), had apparently described her as 'a parrot with a tongue of zinc' (Sitwell 1948, p.30).

It is worth noting Mrs Sitwell's (Colvin 1922) own memory of her first meeting with RLS:

> '...I saw a slim youth in a black velvet jacket and straw hat, with a knapsack on his back, walking up the avenue. 'Here is your cousin,' I said to Mrs Babbington; and she went out through the open French Window to meet him and bring him in. For a few moments he talked rather shyly to us about his long walk from Bury St Edmunds in the heat; and then my little boy, who was with me and had been staring with solemn eyes at Louis, suddenly went up to him and said, 'If you will come with me, I'll show you the moat; we fish there sometimes.' Louis rather jumped at this, and the two boys (for RLS did not look anything like his twenty-three years) went out together hand in hand, and came back in a little while evidently fast friends. From that moment Louis was at his ease, and before twenty-four hours were over the little boy's mother was a fast friend too of RLS, and remained so to the end of his life.' (p.87)

Chaste, maternal but perhaps a trifle disingenuous – the temperate friendliness of Mrs Sitwell's memory seems belied by the passionate correspondence (of which we have only one half), that ensued over the following years. Manuscript 99 in the National Library of Scotland, contains 102 letters written to Mrs Sitwell, most of which were penned in the first two years of their acquaintance. Replete with confessional detail, they offer us a unique insight into the state of the young Stevenson's mind; his relationship with Fanny deepening as the volatile conflict with his parents unfolds.

In September, his father was absent on a business trip, and this provided for a lull in hostilities. '...my mother and I wondered about for two hours', Louis wrote to Mrs Sitwell (Booth and Mehew 1994, pp.304–327), 'We had lunch together and were very merry over what the people in the restaurant would think of us – mother and son they could not suppose us to be; and I think we were throughout good friends' (19th September). Almost immediately the roller-coaster of their relationship took a dip, 'she is quite cold and unresponsive' he complains, 'there is a trial of nervous strength going on between us' (25th September). Then, perhaps as an act of reparation she presents Louis with a small gift, which his father is said to covet for himself. 'I was going to give it up to him', Louis writes, 'but she would not allow me. Besides this she wrote me a very kind letter. There may be better times in that. Still it is always a pic-nic on a volcano' (2nd October).

It is difficult to overestimate the emotional intensity of Stevenson's conflict with his parents at this time, which seemed to take on the proportions of a life and death struggle. Pulled by filial love and remorse —'I cannot help getting friendly with my father (whom I do like)' (22nd September) he writes, and repelled by the obdurateness of paternal authority, he seems to have been caught in a no-win situation. 'My father and I together can get just about a year through in half an hour' (23rd September), he says, and again 'I am killing my father – he told me tonight (by the way that I have alienated utterly my mother) – and this is the result of my attempt to start fresh and fair and to do my best for all of them' (22nd September).

Stevenson obviously felt badly misjudged by his father – no wonder his favourite words in literature were spoken by the loyal Kent (McLynn 1993) whose unimpeachable devotion King Lear had spurned:

> 'O, let him pass! he
> hates him much
> that would upon the rack of this tough world
> stretch him out longer.' (p.276)

In due course, having escaped to the South of France on medical advice, Stevenson plucked up courage to confront his father in a letter. He asserted that henceforth he was to be 'his own man'. Thomas's response was as unexpected in its speed as it was in its content – a telegram by return of post – 'quite satisfied with your letter – keep mind easy, will write.' So far from understanding Louis's position, Thomas had become convinced that his son was on the verge of a mental breakdown. But Louis's sense of uneasy bittersweet triumph over his father's apparent capitulation can be gauged from the ensuing anecdote he relates to Mrs Sitwell. It seems like a kind of allegory, and concerns his encounter with an English dwarf who had befriended him ten years previously when both were the same size. 'It was astonishing how much I had grown', Stevenson writes, 'In opening the door to let him out, I passed my arm thoughtlessly right over his head. Poor fellow the meeting must have been painful for him. When he last knew me, I was something pleasant for him to be with; when he was gone with me alone, he might forget that there was anyone else in the world of different size. And now to find me so changed, to find a sneer where he had been used to see a sort of silent consolation – he must have felt his heart rather wrung.'

Stevenson's voluminous letters to Fanny permit no doubt that he had fallen passionately in love, but a striking development occurs around the end of 1874, which so graphically expresses his sense of exclusion from the parental couple, his belated awareness and sense of betrayal by his mother's unfaithfulness to him; and his substitution of Fanny Sitwell into the mother/lover elision, that I cannot forbear to include it. Where earlier she had been Madonna or Consuelo to him, Stevenson (Booth and Mehew 1994) now insists and henceforth never fails to address her as 'mother'. 'You do not know', he writes, 'perhaps – I do not think I knew perhaps myself, until I thought it out today – how dear a hope, how sorry a want, this has been for me. For my mother is my father's wife; the children of lovers are orphans…and he signs, 'darling mother your son' (11th January 1875, p.102)

The extent to which he had turned away from his actual mother, and the confusion in his mind regarding feelings toward mothers in general, is underlined in a letter he wrote to Fanny the following year:

Dear Mother,

…I long to be with you most ardently, and I long to put my arms about your neck and kiss you, and then sit down with my head on your knees and have a long talk, and feel you smoothing my hair: I long for all that, as one longs for – for nothing else that I can think of. And yet, that is all – It is not a bit like what I feel for my mother here. But I think it must be what one ought to feel for a mother.

Then he adds as an afterthought, 'that's a lie; nobody loves a mere mother, so much as I love you, Madonna.' And signs, 'Before God, RLS.'

'That proves nothing' someone may jibe. 'How can a conscious rhetorical device adopted by Stevenson in a letter, be adumbrated in evidence of an unconscious oedipal struggle? Moreover idealisation of mothers was a Victorian convention, and adolescent rebelliousness does not necessarily betoken any deep unconscious motivation!'

As is well known, Freud (1897) first became persuaded of the ubiquity of the oedipus situation in the late 1890s. He announced in a letter to his friend Wilhelm Fliess, 'I have found in my own case too [the phenomenon of] being in love with my mother and jealousy of my father, and I now consider it a universal event in early childhood' (p.270). He was convinced by his self-analysis, and in particular one dream where he found himself identified with a patient whom he knew to harbour patricidal wishes. In this dream he subsequently became aware that he had intruded into a railway compartment occupied by an elderly couple, and thus prevented them from indulging, as he delicately put it, in 'the affectionate exchanges they had planned for the night.'

Like Freud, Stevenson was a romantic, fascinated by the 'hidden side' of human nature. For no man lives in the external truth among salts and acids, he tells us in *The Lantern Bearers,* 'but in the warm, phantasmagoric chamber of his brain, with the painted windows and storied walls.' Freud states in his justification for the unconscious in 1915 (Freud 1915c):

> '...all the acts and manifestations, which I notice in myself and do not know how to link up with the rest of my mental life, must be judged as if they belonged to someone else: they are to be explained by a mental life ascribed to this other person.'

But twenty-three years earlier Stevenson, in a prescient letter to FH Myers, had attributed the authorship of dreams, to a part of his mind he designated *the other fellow.*

> 'It was myself who spoke and acted; the other fellow seemed to have no control of the body or the tongue; he could only act through myself, on whom he brought to bear a heavy strain...'

Stevenson paid close attention to his dreams, for he came to rely on them for literary material. It is well known that the idea for Jekyll and Hyde was given to him in a dream by internal homunculi:

> '...who do one half my work for me while I am fast asleep, and in all human likelihood, do the rest for me as well, when I am wide awake and fondly suppose I do it for myself. That part which is done while I am sleeping is the Brownies' part beyond contention; but that which is done when I am up and about is by no means necessarily mine, since all goes to show the Brownies have a hand in it even then.'

But there is one dream which Stevenson thought particularly psychologically correct, yet somehow unsuitable for story-telling purposes. Perhaps it was too direct and insufficiently transformed, or perhaps it had already been done by someone else! He included it in his essay (Stevenson 1892) 'On Dreams' written shortly after his father's death, when Stevenson was thirty-seven and I would hazard a guess that he actually dreamt it at that time.

'He is the son of a rich, bad tempered and wicked man, who has avoided his father by living abroad for a long time. He discovers on returning to England that his father is remarried to a young wife, who seems to suffer cruelly and to "loathe her yoke". For some reason connected to this marriage (which the dreamer indistinctly understands), it is desirable for father and son to meet. They do so in a desolate sandy country near the sea, whereupon they quarrel and the son, stung by an intolerable insult, murders his father and inherits his estates.

He finds himself living under the same roof as his father's widow, for whom no provision has been made, living a life of broken dialogue, challenging glances and suppressed passion. One day she slips from the house in a veil and he follows her to the site of the crime. She "gropes among the bents" and finds something with her hand which is deadly evidence against the dreamer; but as she holds it up to look at it her foot slips and the dreamer springs to her rescue. He fears she will denounce him, and one day ransacks her room, eventually finding the damning evidence hidden away among her jewels. She discovers him but says nothing, only teasing him with sly allusions the following morning. He bursts out Why did she torture him so? She knew all, she knew he was no enemy to her. At which point she falls upon her knees and with outstretched arms confesses her love for the dreamer, thus precipitating his instantaneous awakening. Once awake, Stevenson became convinced that during the dream he had been innocent of any knowledge of the woman's motive until the final denouement.' (pp. 161–164)

In May 1880, Stevenson married Fanny Osbourne, an American divorcee ten years older than himself, and the mother of three children, one of whom had died in infancy. His parents had been adamantly against the relationship, but on returning to Scotland later that year, his wife struck up an instant rapport with them. 'Of her new family', a close friend wrote, 'the Mrs Robert Louis Stevenson brought thus strangely from far into their midst made an immediate conquest. To her husband's especial happiness, there sprang up between her and his father the closest possible affection and confidence' (McLynn 1993, p.187).

In October the young Stevensons decamped to Switzerland, where Louis was to be treated in a sanatorium in Davos. On the day of arrival, while Fanny was upstairs inspecting the bedrooms, the mistress of the house apparently informed Louis that his 'mother' would be down shortly!

Stevenson's father died in May 1887. Stevenson arrived too late to be recognised by his father, and was unable to attend the funeral due to ill-health. Soon afterwards he sailed for New York, together with his sixty-year-old mother, Fanny and his young stepson Lloyd. Compton Mackenzie (1968) comments:

> From the moment that Stevenson stepped on board the Ludgate Hill, his health improved, there seems to be no doubt that his tuberculosis was not affected by climate but subject to the ups and downs of his mental condition. Skerryvore [the house his father had obtained for them in Bournemouth] had been for him a prison; he was now free. I believe his mother enjoyed the same fresh air of freedom...' (p.38)

Nevertheless, the Stevensons continued to search for an environment more sympathetic to Louis' consumptive troubles. In 1888, they moved to a new sanatorium by Saranac lake in the Adirondack mountains near the Canadian border. Though far away in time and place, it is from here that Louis recalled a cameo, which I think betokens a mellowing of his internal oedipal father.

The memory refers to his youthful days in Paris. He had left the Comedié Francaise full of indignation, after watching a performance of *Demi-Monde*, in which a young woman is ill-treated. On the way downstairs he happened to tread on an old gentleman's toes, turned to apologise, but instead found himself abusing the old man for having applauded the play and calling him a coward.

Laying his hand on my arm, Stevenson recalls, 'the old gentleman responded with a smile that was truly heavenly in temperance, irony, good-nature, and knowledge of the world, "Ah, monsieur, vous êtes bien jeune!"'

Very well then, my sceptical interlocutor concedes, but this pattern of development has no general significance, being restricted to lapsed Viennese Jews and Scottish Calvinists, in the late nineteenth century.

I refer him wearily to William Stephens' stringent anthropological study, *The Oedipus Complex: Cross Cultural Evidence*, (1962), which found persuasive indications of the oedipal configuration in twentieth century Amerindians.

At the end of 1888, having heard Samoa described as a perfect haven for those with respiratory complaints, Stevenson and his family set out to cross the Pacific in a chartered schooner, which turned out to be riddled with dry rot! They reached Samoa in December 1889 where he was to spend the last five years of his life, and acquire the name of Tusitala – story-teller. On Monday December 3rd, 1894, he died suddenly of a cerebral haemorrhage. Arguably responsible for some of the worst lines in English poetry:

> 'The world is so full of a number of things,
> I'm sure we should all be as happy as Kings.' (Stevenson 1885, p.328)

Stevenson was also capable of rising to the heights; his timeless accord with death adorns his tomb on the summit of Mount Vaea:

> 'Under the wide and starry sky,
> Dig the grave and let me lie
> Glad did I live and gladly die,
> And I laid me down with a will.
>
> This be the verse you grave for me;
> Here he lies where he longed to be;
> Home is the sailor, home from the sea,
> And the hunter home from the hill.'

Original Publication Details

Chapter 1

This chapter first appeared in Hinshelwood, R. and Manning, N. (eds) (1979) *Therapeutic Communities: Reflections and Progress.* London: Routledge.

Chapter 2

This paper was originally presented at a symposium on the 'Evaluation of the Treatment of Drug Abusers' in Upsala in June 1979, at the invitation of the Swedish Medical Research Council. It was subsequently published in Acta Psychiatrica Scaninavica (1980) *Supplementum 284,* 62, 52–57.

Chapter 3

This paper was read to the Oxford Psycho-Analytic Group, June 1982. It was subsequently published in *Group Analysis* (1983), 16, 2, 152–157.

Chapter 4

This lecture was first given in an introductory series on Melanie Klein, to students at the Severnside Insitute for Psychotherapy, Bristol University 1983.

Chapter 5

This lecture was first given in an introductory series on Melanie Klein, to students at the Severnside Insitute for Psychotherapy, Bristol University 1983.

Chapter 6

This paper was originally read to a conference on 'Working with Violence', organised by MIND and St Charles Hospital, London in 1985. It was published in the *British Journal of Psychotherapy* (1986), 3, 2, 119–123 and reprinted in *Psycho-analytic Psychotherapy in South Africa (1993).*

Chapter 7

This chapter first appeared in Pearson, G., Treseder, J. and Yelloly, M. (eds) (1988) *Social Work and the Legacy of Freud: Psychoanalysis and its Uses*. London: Macmillan.

Chapter 8

This brief paper was read to the Oxfordshire Occupational Health Group in 1987.

Chapter 9

This paper was based on a talk first given at a scientific meeting of the Royal College of Psychiatrists, Chiltern and Thames Valley Division at Oxford in October 1983. It was subsequently published with Dr Katherine Wilson as co-author in the *British Journal of Psychiatry* (1985), 146, 277–281.

Chapter 10

This chapter first appeared in Tyrer, P. and Stein, G. (eds) (1993) *Personality Disorder Reviewed*. London: Gaskell.

Chapter 11

This paper was read to a meeting of students at the Institute of Psychoanalysis, London 1979. It was subsequently published in the *International Review of Psychoanalysis* (1980), 7, 483–486.

Chapter 12

This paper is based on a talk first given in the Department of Psychiatry, University of Oxford, June 1983. It was subsequently published in the *International Review of Psychoanalysis (1984), 11, 119–206*.

Chapter 13

This essay first appeared in *Encounter,* December 1988

Chapter 14

This essay first appeared in *Encounter,* July/August 1989.

Chapter 15

This essay first appeared in *Encounter,* April 1990.

Chapter 15

This essay first appeared in *Encounter,* April 1990.

Chapter 16

This previously unpublished lecture was given to the Oxford Psychotherapy Society in November 1993.

References

Abraham, K. (1924a) *Selected Papers*. London: Hogarth Press 1973.

Abraham, K. (1924b) 'Short study of the development of the libido.' In *Selected Papers*. London: Hogarth Press 1973.

Agerholm, L. (1980) Working closely with the family practitioner; unpublished paper given at *International Congress of Psychiatric Nursing for the Eighties*, Imperial College. September, 1980.

Allison, R.B. (1984) 'Difficulties in diagnosing the multiple personality syndrome in a death penalty case.' *International Journal of Clinical and Experimental Hypnosis 32*, 2, 102–17.

Alvarez, A. (1971) *The Savage God*. London: Weidenfeld and Nicholson.

Alvarez, A. (1989) 'A poet and her myths.' *The New York Review of Books*, 28 September.

American Psychiatric Association (1968) *Diagnostic and Statistical Manual of Mental Disorders* (second edition). Washington, DC: American Psychiatric Association.

American Psychiatric Association (1980) *Diagnostic and Statistical Manual of Mental Disorders* (third edition). (DSM-III). Washington, DC: American Psychiatric Association.

American Psychiatric Association (1987) *Diagnostic and Statistical Manual of Mental Disorders* (third edition, revised) (DSM-III-R). Washington, DC: American Psychiatric Association.

Argyris, C. (1970) *Intervention Theory and Method*. Reading, MA: Addison-Wesley.

Bion, N.R. (1973) *Brazilian Lectures*. Sao Paulo: Imago Editora.

Bion, N.R. (1977) *Seven Servants*. New York: Aronson.

Bion, W.R. (1952) 'Group dynamics: a review.' *International Journal of Psychoanalysis 33*, 235–247.

Bion, W.R. (1959) 'Attacks on linking.' In *Second Thoughts*. New York: Jason Aronson. 1967.

Bion, W.R. (1961) *Experiences in Groups*. London: Tavistock.

Bliss, E.L. (1980) 'Multiple personalities: a report of 14 cases with implications for schizophrenia and hysteria.' *Archives of General Psychiatry 37*, 1388–1397.

Boor, M. (1982) 'The multiple personality epidemic.' *Journal of Nervous and Mental Disease 170*, 302–304.,

Breuer, J. and Freud, S. (1893–95) 'Studies on hysteria.' *Standard Edition, Vol.2*, (reprinted 1955). London: Hogarth Press.

Brook, A. (1978) 'An aspect of community mental health: consultative work with general practice teams.' *Health Trends 10*, 37–39.

Brown, G. (1972) *The Mental Hospital as an Institution*. Paper read at 2nd symposium on Psychiatric Epidemiology, Mannheim

Bugliosi, V. and Gentry, C. (1974) *The Manson Murders: An Investigation into Motive*. London: Bodley Head.

Carr, H. and Leared, J. (1973) 'The effect on a child of a mother who though physically present was emotionally unavailable.' In R. Gosling (ed) *Support, Innovation and Autonomy*. London: Tavistock.

Caudill, W.A. (1958) *The Psychiatric Hospital as a Small Society*. Cambridge, MA: Harvard University Press.

Chasseguet-Smirgel, J. (1958) *Creativity and Perversion* London: Free Association Books.

Chodoff, P. (1987) 'More on multiple personality disorder.' *American Journal of Psychiatry 144*, 124.

Clarke, R. and Cornish, D. (1972) *The Controlled Trial in Institutional Research – Paradigm or Pitfall for Penal Evaluators?* London: Home Office Research Studies 15, HMSO.

Coons, P.M. (1986) 'Treatment progress in 20 patients with multiple personality disorder.' *Journal of Nervous and Mental Disease 174*, 715–721.

Coons, P.M. and Milstein, V. (1986) 'Psychosexual disturbances in multiple personality: characteristics, etiology, and treatment.' *Journal of Clinical Psychiatry 47*, 106–110.

Crozier, M. (1965) *The Bureaucratic Phenomenon*. London: Tavistock.

Department of Health and Social Security (1977) *The Role of Psychologists in the Health Services: Report of the Sub-Committee*. London: HMSO.

Dunn, J. and Kendrick, C. (1982) *Siblings*. London: Grant McIntyre.

Edwards, G. (1979) 'British policies on opiate addiction: ten years working of the revised response, and options for the future.' *British Journal of Psychiatry 134*, 1–13.

Ellenberger, H.F. (1970) *The Discovery of the Unconscious*, p.127. London: Allen Lane.

Etzioni, A. (1960) 'Interpersonal and structural factors in the study of mental hospitals.' *Psychiatry 23*, 13–22.

Fahy, T.A. (1988) 'The diagnosis of multiple personality disorder: a critical review.' *British Journal of Psychiatry 153*, 597–606.

Fairbairn, R. (1952) *Psychoanalytic Studies of the Personality.* London: Tavistock.

Fichter, C.G., Kuhlman, D.T., Gruenfield, M.J. *et al.* (1990) 'Decreased episodic violence and increased control of dissociation in a carbamazepine-treated case of multiple personality.' *Biological Psychiatry 27*, 1045–52.

Freud, S. (1895) 'Studies on hysteria.' *Standard Edition, Vol.2.* London: Hogarth Press 1955.

Freud, S. (1897) 'Periodicity and self-analysis.' In J. Masson (ed) (1985) *The Complete Letters of Sigmund Freud to Wilhelm Fliess 1887–1904.* Cambridge, London: Harvard University Press.

Freud, S. (1900) 'The interpretation of dreams.' *Standard Edition, Vol.4.* London: Hogarth Press 1955.

Freud, S. (1905) 'Fragment of an analysis of a case of hysteria.' *Standard Edition, Vol.7.* London: Hogarth Press.

Freud, S. (1910) 'The psycho-analytic view of psychogenic disturbance of vision' *Standard Edition, Vol.11.* London: Hogarth Press.

Freud, S. (1912a) 'The dynamics of transference.' *Standard Edition, Vol.12.* London: Hogarth Press.

Freud, S. (1912b) 'Formulations on the two principles of mental functioning.' *Standard Edition, Vol.12*, p.219. London: Hogarth Press (1958).

Freud, S. (1914) 'Remembering, repeating and working through.' *Standard Edition, Vol.12.* London: Hogarth Press.

Freud, S. (1915a) Instincts and their vicissitudes.' *Standard Edition, Vol.14.* London: Hogarth Press.

Freud, S. (1915b) 'Repression.' *Standard Edition, Vol.14.* London: Hogarth Press.

Freud, S. (1915c) 'The unconscious.' *Standard Edition, Vol.14* (1955). London: Hogarth Press.

Freud, S. (1916) 'Criminals from a sense of guilt.' *Standard Edition, Vol.14.* London: Hogarth Press.

Freud, S. (1917) 'Mourning and melancholia.' *Standard Edition, Vol.14.* London: Hogarth Press.

Freud, S. (1923) 'The ego and the id.' *Standard Edition, Vol.19* (reprinted 1985). London: Hogarth Press.

Freud, S. (1924) 'The economic problem of masochism.' *Standard Edition, Vol.19.* London: Hogarth Press.

Freud, S. (1926) 'The question of lay analysis.' *Standard Edition, Vol.20*, p.226. London: Hogarth Press.

Freud, S. (1930) 'Civilization and its discontents.' *Standard Edition, Vol.21*. London: Hogarth Press.

Freud, S. (1932) 'The dissection of the psychical personality.' *Standard Edition, Vol.22*, p.78. London: Hogarth Press.

Freud, S. (1933) 'New introductory lectures on psychoanalysis.' *Standard Edition, Vol.22*. London: Hogarth Press.

Freud, S. (1940) 'An outline of psychoanalysis.' *Standard Edition, Vol.23*. London: Hogarth Press.

Freud, S. (1985) *The Complete Letters of Sigmund Freud to Wilhelm Fliess 1887–1904.* (Edited by J. Masson). London: Harvard University Press.

Freud, S. and Einstein, A. (1933) 'Why war?' *Standard Edition, Vol.24*. London: Hogarth Press.

Goffman, E. (1961) *Asylums.* New York: Doubleday and Harmondsworth: Penguin. (1968)

Gouldner, A. (1954) *Patterns of Industrial Bureaucracy.* New York: Free Press.

Graham, H. and Scher, M. (1976) 'Social work and general practice: a report of a three year attachment.' *Journal of the Royal College of General Practitioners, 26*, 86.

Greenblatt, M. (1972) 'Administrative psychiatry.' *American Journal of Psychiatry 129*, 373–386.

Greenblatt, M., Levinson, D. and Williams, R. (eds) (1957) *The Patient and the Mental Hospital.* New York: Free Press.

Heimann, P. (1969) 'Counter-transference.' *British Journal of Medical Psychology 33*, 9–15.

Herzog, A. (1984) 'On multiple personality: comments on diagnosis, etiology, and treatment.' *International Journal of Clinical and Experimental Hypnosis 32*, 210—21.

Hilberg, R. (1961) *The Destruction of the European Jews.* London: Allen.

Holbrook, S. (1988) *Sylvia Plath: Poetry and Existence. London/Atlantic Highlands, NJ: Athlone Press.*

Isaacs, S. (1952) *The Nature and Function of Phantasy in Developments in Psychoanalysis.* (Edited by M. Klein, *et al*). London: Hogarth.

James, M. (1960) 'Premature ego development: some observations on disturbances in the first three months of life.' *International Journal of Psychoanalysis 41*, 258–294.

Jaques, E. (1955) 'Social systems as a defence against persecutory and depressive anxiety.' In M. Klein (ed) *New Directions in Psychoanalysis.* London: Tavistock.

Johnston, M. (1978) 'The work of a clinical psychologist in primary care.' *Journal of the Royal College of General Practitioners 28*, 661–667.

Jones, M. (1974) 'Psychiatry, systems theory, education and change.' *British Journal of Psychiatry 124*, 75–80.

Kenny, A. (1973) 'Mental health in Plato's republic.' In *The Anatomy of the Soul*, p.8. Oxford: Blackwell.

Kermode, F. (1985) 'Freud and interpretation.' *International Review of Psychoanalysis 12*, 3–12.

Klein, M. (1929) 'Personification in the play of children.' In K. Masud (ed) *Love, Guilt and Reparation*. London: Hogarth Press 1975.

Klein, M. (1930) 'The importance of symbol-formation in the development of the ego.' In K. Masud (ed) *Love, Guilt and Reparation* (p.219–232). London: Hogarth Press (1975).

Klein, M. (1932) 'An obsessional neurosis in a six-year-old girl. In K. Masud (ed) *The Psychoanalysis of Children*. London: Hogarth Press 1975.

Klein, M. (1935) 'A contribution to the psycho-genesis of manic-depressive states.' In *Love, Guilt and Reparation and Other Works 1921–1945*. London: Hogarth Press 1975.

Klein, M. (1936) 'On weaning.' In *Love, Guilt and Reparation*. London: Hogarth Press.

Klein, M. (1940) 'Mourning and its relation to manic-depressive states.' In *Love, Guilt and Reparation and Other Works 1921–1945*. London: Hogarth Press.

Klein, M. (1946) 'Notes on severe schizoid mechanisms'. In K. Masud (ed) *Envy and Gratitude*. London: Hogarth Press 1975.

Klein, M. (1952) 'The origins of transference.' In M. Klein (ed) *Envy and Gratitude and Other Works 1946–1963*. (1975) London: Hogarth Press.

Klein, M. (1955a) 'The psycho-analytic play technique: its history and significance.' In *Envy and Gratitude and Other Works 1946–1963*. London: Hogarth Press 1975.

Klein, M. (1955b) 'On identification.' In *Envy and Gratitude and Other Works. 1946–1963*. London: Hogarth Press 1975.

Klein, M. (1957) 'Envy and gratitude.' In *Envy and Gratitude and Other Works 1946–196s*. London: Hogarth Press 1975.

Klein, M. (1958) 'On the development of mental functioning.' In *Envy and Gratitude*. London: Hogarth Press.

Klein, M. (1961) *Narrative of a Child Analysis*. London: Hogarth Press.

Kluft, R.P (1982) 'Varieties of hypnotic intervention in the treatment of multiple personality.' *American Journal of Clinical Hypnosis 24*, 230–240.

Kluft, R.P. (1985) 'The treatment of multiple personality disorder: current concepts.' *Directions in Psychiatry (New York) 5*, 1–9.

Kluft, R.P. (1987a) 'The simulation and dissimulation of multiple personality disorder.' *American Journal of Clinical Hypnosis 30*, 104–118.

Kluft, R.P. (1987b) 'An update on multiple personality disorder.' *Hospital and Community Psychiatry 38*, 363–373.

Langer, S. (1942) *Philosophy in a New Key.* Cambridge, MA: Harvard University Press.

Larkin, P. (1983) *Required Writing.* London: Faber and Faber.

Leopoldt, H. (1979) 'GP attachment and psychiatric domiciliary nursing.' *Nursing Times, 75,* 14, 57–59.

Lloyd, D. (1964) *The Idea of Law.* p.163. London: Pelican.

Main, T. (1946) 'The hospital as a therapeutic institution.' *Bulletin of the Menninger Clinic 10,* 66.

Marmer, S. (1980) 'Psychoanalysis of multiple personality.' *International Journal of Psycho-Analysis 61,* 439.

Marx, K. (1844) 'Economic and philosophical manuscripts?' In T.B. Bottomore and M. Rubel (ed) *Karl Marx: Selected Writings in Sociology and Social Philosophy.* London: Pelican, 1963.

Meltzer, D. (1973) *Sexual States of Mind.* Perth: Clunie Press, Roland Harris Trust (p.33).

Meltzer, D. (1984) *Dream Life: A Re-Examination of the Psychoanalytical Theory and Technique.* Perth: Clunie Press, Roland Harris Trust.

Menzies, I. (1960) 'A case study in the functioning of social systems as a defence against anxiety.' *Human Relations* 13, 95–101.

Merskey, H. (1992) 'The manufacture of personalities: the production of multiple personality disorder.' *British Journal of Psychiatry 160,* 327–340.

Mitchell, J.K. (1816) 'A double consciousness or duality of person in the same individual.' *Medical Repository 3,* 185–186.

Mitchell, R. (1983) Liaison psychiatry in general practice. *Hospital Medicine 30,* 2, 100–106.

Money Kyrle, R. (1956) 'The world of the unconscious and the world of common sense.' *British Journal of Philosophy of Science 7,* 25.

Orne, M.T., Dinges, D.F. and Orne, E.C. (1984) 'The differential diagnosis of multiple personality disorder in the forensic context.' *International Journal of Clinical and Experimental Hypnosis 32,* 118–167.

Parsons, T. (1957) 'The mental hospital as a type of organisation.' In M. Greenblatt, D. Levinson and R. Williams (eds) *The Patient and the Mental Hospital.* New York: Free Press.

Pines, M. (1990) 'An English Freud.' *Psychoanalytic Psychotherapy 5*, 1, 1–9.

Plath, A.S. (1976) *Sylvia Plath: Letters Home.* London: Faber and Faber.

Plath, S. (1981) *Collected Poems.* London: Faber and Faber

Prince, M. (1920) 'Miss Beauchamp: the psychogenesis of multiple personality.' *Journal of Abnormal Psychology 16*, 67–137.

Racker, H. (1968) *Transference and Counter-transference.* New York: International University Press.

Reed, J. (1989) *Madness the Price of Poetry.* London?: Peter Owen.

Ricoeur, P. (1970) *Freud and Philosophy.* London: Yale University Press.

Rilke, R.M. (1967) 'Autumn 1913' from *Poems to Night.* In *Selected Works* (translated J.B. Leishman). London: Hogarth Press.

Robinson, J. (1965) 'Mother–infant interaction from birth to twelve months: two case studies.' In B.M. Foss (ed) *Determinants of Infant Behaviour III.* London: Methuen.

Rosenfeld, H. (1962) 'The superego and the ego-ideal.' *International Journal of Psycho-Analysis 43*, 258–263.

Rosenfeld, H. (1971) 'A clinical approach to the psycho-analytic theory of the life and death instincts.' *International Journal of Psycho-Analysis 52*, 169–178.

Ross A. and Gahan M. (1988) 'Techniques in the treatment of multiple personality disorder.' *American Journal of Psychotherapy 42*, 40–52.

Ross, C. (1987) 'Inpatient treatment of multiple personality disorder.' *Canadian Journal of Psychiatry 32*, 779–781.

Rycroft, C. (1985) 'The present state of Freudian psychoanalysis.' In P. Fuller (ed) *Psychoanalysis and Beyond.* London: Chatto and Windus.

Ryle, G. (1949) *The Concept of Mind.* London: Hutchinson.

Science (1886) 'Editorial.' *Science 7*, 169, 397–399.

Snow, C.P. (1959) *The Two Cultures and the Scientific Revolution* (1962 edition). London: Cambridge University Press.

Spence, D. (1982) *Narrative Truth and Historical Truth.* New York: Norton.

Sperry, R. (1965) 'Brain bisection and the mechanisms of consciousness.' In J.C. Eccles (ed) *The Brain and Conscious Behaviour.* New York: Springer.

Stanton, A. and Schwartz, M. (1954) *The Mental Hospital.* New York: Basic Books.

Steiner, J. (1981) 'Perverse relationships between parts of the self: a clinical illustration.' *International Journal of Psycho-Analysis 162*, 241–251.

Stephens, W. (1962) *The Oedipus Complex: Cross Cultural Evidence.* New York: Free Press.

Stevenson, A. (1989) *Bitter Fame: A Life of Sylvia Plath.* London: Viking.

Stevenson, A. (1989) 'Hot Wind, Hard Rain.' *Poetry Review 79*, 2.

Strachey, J. (1934) 'The nature of the therapeutic action of psychoanalysis.' *International Journal of Psycho-Analysis 50*, 275–291.

Strauss, A., Schatzman, L., Erlich, D., Bucher, R. and Sabshin, M. (1963) 'The hospital and its negotiated order.' In E. Freidson (ed) *The Hospital in Modern Society*. New York: Free Press.

Szasz, T.S. (1963) 'The concept of transference.' *International Journal of Psychoanalysis 44*, 432–443.

Tantam, D. (1990) 'Iatrogenic Identities.' *British Journal of Psychiatry Review of Books 1*, 19–21.

Temperley, J. (1978) Psychotherapy in the setting of general medical practice. *British Journal of Medical Psychology 51*, 139–145.

The Times (1990) '"Three faces" of Sarah give evidence.' *Times*, November 9.

Vaillant, G. (1973) 'A twenty-year follow-up of new york narcotic addicts.' *Archives of General Psychiatry 29*, 237–241.

Wagner-Martin, L. (1988a) *Sylvia Plath: A Biography*. London: Chatto and Windus.

Wagner-Martin, L. (ed) (1988b) *Sylvia Plath: The Critical Heritage*. London: Routledge.

Watkins, J.G. (1984) 'The Bianchi (L.A. hillside strangler) case: sociopath or multiple personality.' *International Journal of Clinical and Experimental Hypnosis 32*, 86.

Weber, M. (1948) 'Bureaucracy.' In H. Gerth and C. Wright Mills (eds) *From Max Weber*. London: Routledge and Kegan Paul.

Whyte, L.L. (1978) *The Unconscious Before Freud*. London: Julian Friedmann.

Whyte, L.L. (1979) *The Unconscious Before Freud*. London: Julian Friedmann.

Williams, P. (1983) Unpublished communication. *General Practice Research Unit, Institute of Psychiatry, London*.

Wilson, C. (1985) *A Criminal History of Mankind*. London: Panther.

Wilson, S. (1978) 'The effect of treatment in a therapeutic community on intravenous drug abuse.' *British Journal of Addiction 73*, 407–411.

Wilson, S. and Mandelbrote, B. (1978) 'Drug rehabilitation and criminality: factors related to conviction after treatment in a therapeutic community.' *British Journal of Criminology 18*, 381–386.

Wisdom, J. (1984) 'What is left of psychoanalytic theory?' *International Review of Psychoanalysis 11*, 313–326.

World Health Organization (1953) *Report of Expert Committee on Mental Health*. Geneva: World Health Organization.

World Health Organization (1973) *Psychiatry and Primary Medical Care Report of Working Group.* Copenhagen: World Health Organization.

World Health Organization (1987) *The ICD-10 classification of Mental and Behavioural Disorders.* Geneva: World Health Organization.

Yablonsky, L. (1965) *The Tunnel Back.* New York: Macmillan.

Literary References

Andersen, H.C. (1843) 'The nightingale.' In S. Dahl and H. Topsøe-Jensen (eds) *Six Fairy Tales by the Danish Writer Hans Christian Andersen.* Copenhagen: Det Berlingske Bogtrykkeri 1955.

Balfour, G. (1901) *The Life of Robert Louis Stevenson.* London: Methuen.

Booth, B. and Mehew, E. (eds) *The Letters of Robert Louis Stevenson (1994).* Newhaven, London: Yale University Press.

Bowra, M. (1961) *The Romantic Imagination.* London: Oxford University Press.

Carey, J. (1993) 'Dull and void.' *The Sunday Times* 9th May.

Carlyle, T. (1843) 'Past and present.' In H.D. Traill (ed) *Centenary Edition of Carlyle's Works.* London 1897

Carpenter, H. (1988) *A Serious Character: The Life of Ezra Pound.* London: Faber and Faber.

Casillo, R. (1988) *The Genealogy of Demons: Anti-Semitism, Fascism, and the Myths of Ezra Pound.* Evanston, Ill: Northwestern University Press.

Christ, C. (1976) 'Aggression and providential death in George Eliot's fiction.' *Novel 9,* 130–140.

Cohn, N. (1967) *Warrant for Genocide: The Myth of the Jewish World-Conspiracy and the Protocols of the Elders of Zion.* (Revised 1981). London: Eyre and Spottiswoode.

Colvin, F. (1922) 'My first meeting with RLS.' In R. Masson (ed) *I Can Remember Robert Louis Stevenson (1922).* Edinburgh: W and R Chambers.

Colvin, S. (1901) *The Letters of Robert Louis Stevenson.* Edinburgh: W and R Chambers.

Corbière, T. (1954) 'Gens de mer.' In C.S. MacIntyre (ed) *Selections from Les Amours Jaunes* (pp.147–151). Berkeley, CA: University of California Press.

Cross, J. (1884) *George Eliot's Life* (p.9). London: Blackwood.

Donne, J. (1553–1601) 'The flea.' In J. Hayward (ed) *John Donne.* Harmondsworth: Penguin 1950.

Eliot, G. (1858) 'Mr Gilfil's love story.' In *Scenes of Clerical Life.* London: Virago Press 1985.

Eliot, G. (1858) *Scenes of Clerical Life.* Harmondsworth: Penguin English Library 1973.

Eliot, G. (1871) *Middlemarch*. Harmondsworth: Penguin English Library 1965.

Eliot, G. (1876) *Daniel Deronda*. Harmondsworth: Penguin English Library 1967.

Eliot, G. (1878) *The Lifted Veil*. London: Virago Press 1985.

Eliot, G. (1860) *The Mill on the Floss*. Harmondsworth: Penguin English Library 1979.

Eliot, G. (1863) *Romola*. Harmondsworth: Penguin English Library 1980.

Eliot, G. (1866) *Felix Holt*. Harmondsworth: Penguin English Library 1972.

Eliot, G. (1954) *Letters*. (Edited by G.S. Haight.) New Haven, CT: Yale University Press.

Eliot, T.S. (1935) *Time and Tide*, 5th January.

Eliot, T.S. (1936) unsigned review of *The Yellow Spot*. In *The Criterion 15*, 759–60.

Eliot, T.S. (1954) *Selected Poems*. London: Faber and Faber.

Eliot, T.S. (1959) 'Little Gidding.' *Four Quartets*. London: Faber and Faber.

Eliot, T.S. (1971) *The Waste Land: A Facsimile and Transcript*. (Edited by Valerie Eliot). London: Faber and Faber.

Friedländer, S. (1984) *Reflections of Nazism: An Essay on Kitsch and Death*. New York: Harper and Row.

Fuller Torrey, E. (1984) *The Roots of Treason and the Secrets of St. Elizabeth's*. London: Sidgwick and Jackson.

Gass, W.H. (1989) 'Review of a serious character'. *The Times Literary Supplement*, 13–19 January.

Gilbert, S. (1979) *The Madwoman in the Attic*. New Haven, CT: Yale University Press.

Graham, A.C. (1988) Letter in *The Times Literary Supplement*, 18–24 November.

Haight, G. (1968) *George Eliot: A Biography*. Oxford: Claredon Press.

Hanson, L. and Hanson, E. (1952) *Marian Evans and George Eliot*. Oxford: Oxford University Press.

Homberger, E. (ed) (1972) *Ezra Pound: The Critical Heritage*. London: Routledge and Kegan Paul. Quoting Pound, 'Reply.' *New English Review* October 12, 1933, Pound, Guide to Kulchur, p.186.

Hopkins, G.M. (1970) 'The Wreck of the Deutschland stanza I.' In W.H. Gardner and N.H. MacKenzie (eds) *The Poems of Gerard Manley Hopkins*. London: Oxford University Press.

James, H. (1876) 'Daniel Deronda. A conversation.' In F.R. Leavis (ed) *The Great Tradition: George Eliot–Henry James–Joseph Conrad*. London: Chatto and Windus, 1948.

Keats, J. (ed) (1906) *The Poems of John Keats* (Everyman's Library Ed. Ernest Rhys). London: J.M. Dent and Sons.

Leavis, F.R. (1948) *The Great Tradition: George Eliot–Henry James–Joseph Conrad.* London: Chatto and Windus.

Mackenzie, C. (1968) *Robert Louis Stevenson.* London: Morgan-Grampian.

Masson, F. (1922) 'Louis Stevenson in Edinburgh.' In R. Masson (ed) *I Can Remember Robert Louis Stevenson.* Edinburgh: W and R Chambers.

McLynn, F. (1993) *Robert Louis Stevenson.* London: Hutchinson.

Norrington, A.L.P. (ed) (1968) *The Poems of Arthur Hugh Clough.* Oxford: Clarendon Press.

Orwell, G. (1946) 'Politics and the English language'. In *Inside the Whale.* Harmondsworth: Penguin 1957.

Owens, L. (ed) *The Complete Brothers Grimm Fairy Tales.* Avenel: USA.

Pound, E. (1965) *The Cantos.* New York: New Directions.

Ricks, C. (1988) *T. S. Eliot and Prejudice.* London: Faber and Faber.

Sade, Marquis de (1966) *The 120 Days of Sodom and Other Writings.* New York: Random House.

Sitwell, O. (1948) *Great Morning.* London: Macmillan.

Stephen, L. (1902) *George Eliot.* London: Macmillan.

Stevenson, R.L. (1866) 'Student days at Edinburgh.' In S. Colvin (ed) *The Letters of Robert Louis Stevenson (1901).* Edinburgh: W. and R. Chambers.

Stevenson, R.L. (1873) 'Ordered south: Mentone October 1873–April 1874 (Friday 28 November, p.380).' In B. Booth and E. Mehew (eds) *The Letters of Robert Louis Stevenson (1994).* Newhaven, London: Yale University Press.

Stevenson, R.L. (1885) *A Child's Garden of Verses in Poems (1913).* London: Chatto and Windus.

Stevenson, R.L. (1886) *The Strange Case of Dr Jekyll and Mr Hyde.* p.82. (reprinted 1979) London: Penguin.

Stevenson, R.L. (1888) 'The United States again: winter in the Adironalacks August 1887–October 1888 (letter to William Archer).' In S. Colvin (eds) *The Letters of Robert Louis Stevenson (1901).* Edinburgh: W and R Chambers.

Stevenson, R.L. (1889) *The Master of Ballantyne. A Winters Tale.* Oxford: Oxford University Press (1988).

Stevenson, R.L. (1892a) Letter to FH Myers quoted in *The Subliminal Consciousness,* Proceedings of the Society for Psychical Research.

Stevenson, R.L. (1892b) 'On dreams.' In S. Colvin (ed) *Across the Plains (1913).* London: Chatto and Windus.

Stevenson, R.L. (1892) 'The Lantern Bearers.' In S. Colvin (ed) *Across the Plains (1913).* London: Chatto and Windus.

Stevenson, R.L. (1896) *Weir of Hermiston: An Unfinished Romance*. London: Chatto and Windus.

Stevenson, R.L. (1913) 'A chapter on dreams.' In S. Colvin (ed) *Across the Plains*. London: Chatto and Windus.

Uglow, J. (1987) *George Eliot*. London: Virago.

Wilde, O. (1898) 'The ballad of reading gaol.' In *The Soul of Man and Prison Writings*. Oxford: Oxford University Press 1990.

Yeats, W.B. (1917) 'Per amica silenta lunae: anima hominis.' In *Mythologies* (1959, 1969, p.331). London: Macmillan.

Subject Index

Author Index